How to get your
LAWN
OFF
GRASS

A NORTH AMERICAN GUIDE TO TURNING OFF THE WATER TAP AND GOING NATIVE

CAROLE RUBIN

HARBOUR PUBLISHING

Published by
HARBOUR PUBLISHING
P.O. Box 219, Madeira Park, BC Canada V0N 2H0
www.harbourpublishing.com

Cover and interior design by Martin Nichols
Cover photographs: Background image: Northern maidenhair fern (*Adiantum pedatum*), Roberts Creek, BC, by Kai Goodwin; top right, woodland path, Rich Cove Forest, Pawling, NY, courtesy Quaker Hill Native Garden; bottom right, adobe house and garden, Las Vegas, Nevada and, bottom left, garden and deck, Dallas, Texas, by Andy Wasowski
Some of Andy Wasowski's photographs are from the following books: *Native Texas Gardens* by Sally Wasowski and Andy Wasowski. Houston: Gulf Publishing, 1997; *Native Landscaping from El Paso to LA* by Sally Wasowski with Andy Wasowski. Chicago: Contemporary Books, 2000; *Gardening With Native Plants of the South* by Sally Wasowski with Andy Wasowski. Dallas: Taylor Publishing, 1994; *Gardening with Prairie Plants* by Sally Wasowski. Minneapolis: University of Minnesota Press, 2001.
Chris Young's photographs are from *The State Journal-Register*, Springfield, Illinois, Summer, 2001
Printed in Canada
Second Printing, 2002

THE CANADA COUNCIL | LE CONSEIL DES ARTS
FOR THE ARTS | DU CANADA
SINCE 1957 | DEPUIS 1957

Harbour Publishing acknowledges the financial support of the Government of Canada through the Book Publishing Industry Development Program (BPIDP) and the Canada Council for the Arts, and the Province of British Columbia through the British Columbia Arts Council, for its publishing activities.

National Library of Canada Cataloguing in Publication Data

Rubin, Carole.
   How to get your lawn off grass

   ISBN 1-55017-259-X

   1. Organic gardening. 2. Lawns. 3. Native plant gardening. I. Title.
SB453.5.R822 2002   635.9'87   C2001-911664-0

For Isabel, Shannon, Amina, and Bill

Table of Contents

Preface

When I first started gardening, Carole Rubin's book *How to Get Your Lawn and Garden Off Drugs* was my most valued, thumbed-through guide, telling me everything I needed to know to get started on the path to organic gardening.

Now, with *How to Get Your Lawn Off Grass*, Rubin's commitment to caring for the earth has grown naturally (indeed, organically) into a passion for gardening with native plants. She brings her trademark blend of wry humour, gutsy opinions and cheerful encouragement to the subject, reminding us that everything we do in the garden—our plant choices, our maintenance techniques—has an impact on the world. And she offers us the information we need to make that impact positive.

Rubin's focus is water conservation, but the message contained in this book extends far beyond that worthy goal: when we garden with native plants, not only are we saving precious water by using plants adapted to local conditions, we're also promoting biodiversity, creating habitat for wildlife and connecting with the natural features of our unique bioregions. Think of how different—for the better!—our world would be if the gardens Rubin describes were as common as lawns are now...If more people embraced the environmental goals at the heart of this book...Rubin is an inspired and inspiring guide on that path to the future.

—Lorraine Johnson

Lorraine Johnson is the author of a number of books about native plant gardening, including *100 Easy-to-Grow Native Plants for Canadian Gardens* and *Grow Wild! Native Plant Gardening in Canada*.

ACKNOWLEDGEMENTS

Every single person and organization that I contacted in preparation for this book opened my eyes to the wonderful spirits of those in the native plant community. Photographs, information, stories, advice, introductions ("You should talk to so-and-so! Let me call for you!") and encouragement were offered spontaneously and with good grace, each source content to be "paid" with the knowledge that one more person, one more book, would be spreading the word.

I want to acknowledge all of the Native Plant Societies in North America, run by volunteers who have lives and families yet who constantly keep meetings and information lines open to anyone seeking information about native plants.

Native plant organizations, such as The Wild Ones Natural Landscapers, provide a terrific service in many states to any who require their help in getting started with native plants, right down to providing their handbook (for free!) on the internet.

Two experts in the field of native plant gardening: Lorraine Johnson, of Ontario, and Sally Wasowski, of New Mexico, gave extensively and graciously of their time and vast knowledge to the total stranger who sent them e-mails literally out of the blue. I have yet to meet either in person, and plan to remedy that situation as soon as possible.

Finally, I want to thank all the native plant gardeners out there, quietly restoring native habitat and meeting the challenges of being on the leading edge, challenging neighbours' and municipalities' concepts of what a yard should be, especially Carol Coker of Pasco, Washington, and Douglas Counter of Toronto, Ontario.

To all of you, those that came before, those that will come after, I give my gratitude for your work, and for sharing so freely of yourselves.

Introduction

by Sally Wasowski

It was in 1984 when my husband Andy and I first began to write books and give talks on the advantages of landscaping with native plants. After all, native plants flourish on their own without help from humans.

They can grow without aid from a garden hose. My mentor, Benny J. Simpson, the horticulturist in residence at the Agricultural Division of the Texas Research Foundation in Renner, Texas, used to say: "Native plants are beautiful and horticulturally worthy, but eventually everyone will use them whether they want to or not, because of the lack of water."

I knew exactly what he meant. Some of my earliest memories are of the seven-year drought in the 1950s. I remember Dallas streets lined with brown lawns. I remember my grandmother washing and rinsing dishes in the same one inch of water. I remember my mother closing all the windows when the sky turned brown and afterwards cleaning miniature dunes of sand off the windowsills.

In the 1980s, we had more than seasonal cycles of drought to contend with. We had a world-wide population explosion. Furthermore, in North America, plumbing and cheap water made the use of large amounts of water so easy and financially painless that gardens, lawns, swimming pools, golf courses and manufacturers were wasting water at a rate that would have been unimaginable before World War II.

There were some people speaking out that water was a finite resource and that our earth could not sustain our present rate of wastefulness and pollution. But most people were having too much fun to think of the future. They were sure that if and when disaster struck, "modern technology" would rescue the day.

As water departments spread information on xeriscaping and asked municipalities to let them raise water rates to slow consumption, there were outcries from the public. I have spoken to many people who were convinced that there was enough water for everyone forever and that the water department was lying and using scare tactics to try to gouge money out of water users.

Now, nearly twenty years later, with continued population growth, more and more cities are experiencing water shortages and water rationing. Are our landscapes reflecting a new awareness of the need to conserve water? Alas, no. Our neighbourhoods are still carpeted with lawns. Garden centres and nurseries still sell more water-guzzling exotics than native plants. The word "xeriscape" has been twisted. It no longer means drought-tolerant plants that, once established, can live on rainfall alone. It often refers to plants that need watering once or twice a week to stay alive!

In many places where "native" plants are sold, there is no attention paid to where the plants are actually native. Sweetgums are sold in Arizona as "native" plants, even though sweetgums do not grow on their own there, but in the Deep South where the average rainfall is 45 inches more a year than it is in the Desert Southwest.

Those of us speaking out for native plants and water conservation used to talk on the basis of common sense and intuition. But today that intuition is backed by solid research and definite numbers. If you are still one of the ostrich people who would prefer to see no water shortages, try reading the first few chapters of this book. See how much more "drinking water" you want to pour on your lawn, when there are attractive and healthier alternatives. Maybe you will not only be convinced yourself. Maybe you'll use the facts inside these covers to convince others. I'm always hopeful.

Sally Wasowski is a landscape designer and author of nine books on gardening with native plants.

CHAPTER ONE

Water, Water, Everywhere

Five Facts And A Truth:

THE FACTS FIRST:

- Human beings cannot survive without clean, safe water to drink.
- Only one half of 1% of the water on the planet is drinkable.
- The water supply is finite. As our population continues to grow out of control, the amount of available water diminishes.
- 1.3 *billion* people on the planet do not have access to clean drinking water right now.
- Four thousand people die *each day* from water-borne diseases.

NOW THE TRUTH: LAWNS SUCK WATER!

Conventional turf-grass lawns and ornamental exotic gardens (gardens that are planted with species that originated in different climates) are responsible for consuming 60% of daily domestic drinking water used in North America. *Sixty percent* of the one half of 1% of the planet's available, clean drinking water.

Just let that sink in.

An 8- by 12-metre (25- by 40-foot) lawn needs about 38,000 litres (10,000 gallons) of water a summer to keep it green. To keep it the bouncy, vibrant green we have become addicted to, make it 46,000 litres (12,000 gallons) a summer. Of drinking water.

And this "clean" drinking water is rapidly disappearing around the planet, as population explosion, resource extraction, global warming and pollution take their toll. Town after town across North America is finding its water supply gone, or undrinkable due to the presence of high bacteria counts or man-made chemical contamination. In the past year (August 2000–August 2001) we've had news reports of contaminated water supplies all over North America, from Walkerton, Ontario to Lake Tahoe, California. I live in a temperate rain forest, yet more people get sick from contaminated water here than anywhere else in Canada.

Water Business

Most of the lakes in the world are polluted.

This crisis of pollution and the scarcity of clean water are viewed by some as a tremendous business opportunity.

Monsanto, the company that brought you patented and genetically altered vegetable seeds, along with Round-up and other pesticides, is trying to "buy" rights to clean water all over the world, in order to SELL it back to us. This is not a joke! Truth IS stranger than fiction! And there's more:

The World Bank wants to privatize water and establish a trade in water rights.

A California company is suing the Canadian government under the North American Free Trade Agreement (NAFTA) because British Columbia banned water exports. This company is asking for $250 million dollars US in compensation for "lost revenues" because it cannot access BC's water to sell.

Water Wars And Big Sticks

Forty percent of the world's population relies on water originating in a country that is not their own.

In North America, some states are already in legal conflict with their neighbours for rights to the water that flows across their mutual borders.

Malaysia, which supplies about half of Singapore's water, threatened to cut off their supply over criticism of government policies.

Some states in the USA are taking neighbouring states to court over damming and water diversion.

And it is going to get nastier.

Given these facts, should it even be *legal* to consume 60% of our .5% of available water and then contaminate it for a (ahem) LAWN OR FLOWER?

Environmental Refugees

Just ask the environmental refugees of the world, people who have moved their families to a region that, among other things, at the very least has drinkable water. Ask those not able to move, consigned to drink and bathe in contaminated water, or to walk miles each day to get their water for drinking and cooking. Over one billion people on the planet make this daily sojourn.

By 2010, about 2.5 billion people in the world will lack access to clean drinking water. In the United States, 30% of the population will experience severe water shortages by that date.

So water is THE next hot commodity. Something to make money from, something to go to war for, something to use as a political big stick.

After oil, the next global conflicts will be about access to fresh water. As population and demands for water grow, so does the potential for violent conflict. Bet on it.

This lush garden, a mixture of native and non-native plants at a driveway's edge in Boundary Bay, British Columbia, needs no watering even in extreme drought conditions. Native plants include western red cedar (*Thuja plicata*), crane's bill, or Richardson's geranium (*Geranium richardsonii*) and sedge grasses.
Edward van Veenendaal photo

Another Truth: Lawns Pollute!

Runoff from chemical treatment of lawns and gardens itself has seriously compromised ground water supplies everywhere in the United States and Canada.

Several Canadian provincial Ministry of Environment departments have been concerned since the mid-eighties about runoff from lawns and gardens that have been dosed with pesticides and chemical fertilizers. Some municipalities have been practising low- or no-use programs for years, and some are now even making it official by passing non-cosmetic-use bylaws (e.g. Halifax, Nova Scotia). Hundreds more are looking to do the same.

The USA Environmental Protection Agency (EPA) estimates that forty-three million kilograms (ninety-five million pounds) of chemicals are applied to American lawns each year, and that number grows by 6% annually.

That urea-based fertilizer, that combo fertilizer/ weed control, that fungicide for moss, that herbicide for "weeds," that insecticide for ants...where do you think these chemicals go after they are put on your yard?

With the first rain or watering, right into your community's groundwater!

So lawns not only suck water, they actually contaminate it when toxic chemicals are used.

And do the weeds come back after chemical treatment?

Pesticide manufacturers depend upon it.

And does the lawn still go brown and will those exotic flowers wilt and die without yet still more water? Uh-huh.

And is this healthy or even smart?

Lawn Toys Pollute, Too!

Then there's the pollution and resource consumption from lawn mowers, leaf blowers, etc.

The US EPA estimates that a three-and-a-half HP lawn mower pollutes the air in a single mowing with as much exhaust as a new full-sized car driven 560 kilometres (350 miles). They also estimate that the 50 million lawn mowers in the US burn at least 1140 million litres (300 million gallons) of gas per year, and that 76 million litres (20 million gallons) of gasoline and oil are spilled each year, just refuelling lawn-care equipment! That's more than the Exxon Valdez spilled into the Gulf of Alaska in 1989.

And electric mowers, while "cleaner," use power.

Lawns Are Monocultures Begging For Trouble

It's simple. Because lawns are monocultures, or a blend of a few grasses at best, they ATTRACT the problems that plague gardeners. If there is a Kentucky bluegrass-loving insect or disease in your area, and you have a lawn of Kentucky blue, well, you figure it out. Dinner's on!

A drought will decimate a monoculture that is drought sensitive, but will only challenge a small part of a planting of natives that have varying needs.

And native birds, butterflies, bees, and moths that depend on the seeds, berries and flowers of native flora are less likely to visit your Kentucky blue.

Lawns Are Not North American Friendly

The grass plants in your front lawn are almost assuredly created from stock that is not native to your neck of the woods, or even to your hemisphere. Therefore your climate and soil conditions will *never* be optimum for your lawn's health. Your grass plants will always be stressed and more susceptible to disease, pests and severe weather. This means an endless future of very expensive, intense, and environmentally damaging maintenance to keep those exotic grass plants looking "pretty."

This gorgeous patch of bee balm (*Monarda didyma*) in Guelph, Ontario, attracts bees, ruby-throated hummingbirds and monarch butterflies, all of which flock to the nectar that Kentucky bluegrass does not provide.
Brad Peterson photo

And Never A Drop To Drink

Most of the drinking water applied to your lawn never even makes it to the deep roots of your grass plants. Much is lost to evaporation, or, at best, sits on the mat of thatch at the base of the grass leaves, making a nice warm, moist breeding ground for diseases and insects that attack lawns.

And if you, like most North Americans, water too frequently and too shallowly, the water that *does* make it into the soil will only penetrate an inch or two, causing your grass roots to curl up to the surface in search of moisture. This weakens the plants, again, making them more susceptible to problems.

Lawns Need Super Soil

For your lawn to bc its healthiest, the plant roots need to grow to a minimum depth of 20 cm (8 inches) in humus-rich, fertile soil, with good aeration and millions of beneficial organisms that naturally protect the plants from predators. Sound like your yard?

Lawns Speak Volumes But Say So Little About Us

Most towns and cities in North America could be interchangeable. Lots of pavement, lots of buildings, and as Lorraine Johnson has so accurately stated, lots of yards "covered with the botanic equivalent of pavement: lawns." Same trees, same shrubs, same same. Morbid silence. Little or no bird life. Few, if any, butterflies. Sterile. Could be Manitoba, could be Massachusetts, could be Montana. BORING.

Now find and check out a native yard in your area. Cheeps, trills, and squawks of birds, gorgeous butterflies, humming honeybees. Lots of unusual (in fact, usual) trees, shrubs, flowers and ground covers that are not found in any other part of the continent.

Lawns say so little about us. A flat green lawn could be anywhere: Montana, Manitoba, or Massachusetts. Indoor-outdoor carpeting, anyone? This drop-dead gorgeous Dallas, Texas, yard, however, is full of personal expression and plants native to its particular region. Around the deck is a tall autumn grass, Lindheimer muhly (*Muhlenbergia lindheimeri*). The red flowers are Turk's cap (*Malvaviscus drummondii*) and the yellow flowers are Lindheimer senna (*Senna lindheimeriana*).
Andy Wasowski photo

Found only in your part of the world, and a celebration of LIFE.

Clearly, it is time for North Americans to rethink their lawn addiction and its financial and ecological cost.

Some municipalities have banned water use for lawns in the summer, period.

Some governments in North America are already offering financial incentives and technical support to residents to remove their guzzling, polluting lawns and replace them with native plants.

THIS BOOK WILL TELL YOU HOW TO DO JUST THAT: how to cut, roll up and compost your turf-grass lawn and your water-sucking ornamental "exotic" garden plants and replace them with gorgeous native ground covers, flowers, shrubs, trees and grasses that will need no fertilizers, no chemical controls for pests, no mowing and NO WATER after their first year.

But first, let's take a look at this obsession with lawns and fancy flowers from foreign countries, and where the first seeds for that obsession were sown.

CHAPTER TWO

Out Of The Forest
And Onto The Lawn

From the beginning, lawns have meant status and wealth. Here's how it happened.

Africa, Asia, Europe & Great Britain

There are several versions of how lawns got their start. Most sources agree that the clearing of land began with the advent of settled communities in Africa, and later, Europe and Britain, to enable people to see their enemies advancing. There are differing opinions on whether those "enemies" were other humans, wild animals, or nature, herself.

Whatever the fear, forests were cut down, and tall grasses kept short, by early lawn mowers: slaves and the merely poor.

As farming developed, more trees were cut to make way for crops.

As communities and hierarchies became more evolved, the wealthy had more leisure time. They began to keep grass short to provide play areas inside the castle walls, and to cultivate large expanses of non-food-producing areas outside their homes, yards intentionally landscaped with grasses.

Royal and aristocratic grounds had to look splendid to keep up with the social one-upmanship of high society. In the early teens in Europe, and then in England, all flora and fauna that was foreign was sought after to reflect one's wealth and "taste." The more foreign, the better, and the exotic plant trade began in earnest.

In the early eighteenth century, the palace at Versailles had its *tapis vert*, or "green carpet," made entirely of grasses from Asia, designed by one of the early landscape architects, Andre Lenotre. Peacocks and tigers from India prowled well-manicured mega-estates in England and Europe, planted with date palms and African grasses.

As money trickled down to the next layers of society in the mid- to late eighteenth century, new landowners got busy emulating those above them by building estates, and, of course, the biggest lawns possible. "Turf" became an accepted sign of wealth and status.

Into The New World

When Europeans first reached North America, there were no lawns or gardens. The first peoples of eastern North America used natural clearings in the woodlands to grow their crops, moving these "farms" from year to year to maintain healthy soils. Plains Indians burned the native grasses from time to time to encourage buffalo and bison to graze on new shoots that pushed up through the soil after a fire. And on the west coast, fishing, hunting and foraging kept first peoples happy.

The first European farmers to land on America's east coast replaced native annual grasses with grasses and clovers from home, which they believed had a higher nutritive value for grazing animals. In the mid-sixteenth century, clover was a major import to New England.

The east coast was also likely the original foothold for dandelions, plantain and other weeds via the ballast of ships anchored in harbour. Ballast, grazing stock and birds hitchhiking on slave and trade ships spread Bermuda grass and Guinea grass, both natives of Africa, and Kentucky bluegrass, a native of the Middle East, throughout the south before human settlement.

The first North American lawns were planted in New England by wealthy landowners in the late 1700s to copy the aristocracy of England and Europe. These North American properties became "estates." Kentucky bluegrass, which was the darling of the English estate greens, became the favourite lawn grass in North America.

As the lower classes achieved the ability to own land, they were encouraged by the wealthy to plant the mud yards facing the streets with lawns, and to Beautify America.

Then came the suburbs, and lawns were entrenched in our psyche. To have a lawn showed communal wealth, status, and good taste—and defined one's domain. "Turf Wars" were not accidentally named.

And now?

The Great Lawn Questionnaire

In preparing for this book, I informally and unscientifically surveyed two hundred Canadian men and women at random and asked them four questions:

- In five words or less, what does your lawn mean to you?
- In five words or less, what does your flower garden mean to you?
- How would you feel if you were asked to replace your lawn with native trees, shrubs, flowers and grasses or ground covers that need no water once established?
- How would you feel about replacing your existing ornamental landscaping with native trees, shrubs, flowers, grasses and ground covers?

The results were fascinating.

THE MEN SPEAK

What does my lawn mean to me? The men invariably (78%) used words like "pride," "beauty," "peace," and, tellingly, "best in the neighbourhood" when referring to their lawns.

When asked how they felt about their gardens, they were less enthusiastic—and no wonder—only 12% of the men were involved in their creation or care. So they responded with "nice," "pretty, I guess," and "that's my wife's/partner's thing."

In response to a proposal to replace their lawns with native plants, an overwhelming 87% were aghast at the idea for any reason whatsoever, no sir, no ma'am, leave my lawn alone! Responses like "No way!" "Just try it!" and "I'd refuse!" were literally gouged into the paper. Reasons given: "Where will the kids play?" or "I love my new mower!" However, most respondents admitted that their kids weren't allowed to or didn't play on the lawn anyway. Some who gave kids as a reason even admitted that they were kid-less. Interesting.

The most common response to the idea of replacing the gardens with native plants was, "Not my area, ask my partner."

Eric Wold of Eugene, Oregon, calls these native plants HIS beauties, and he never waters. They are: pearly everlasting (*Anaphalis margaritacea*), foreground, Canada goldenrod (*Solidago canadensis*), middle ground, and Douglas spirea (*Spirea douglasii*), background. To the right of the goldenrod is red-osier dogwood (*Cornus sericea*). Eric Wold photo

THE WOMEN SPEAK

In answer to what their lawns meant to them, more than half of the women (58%) were lukewarm, at best. They used words like "too much work," "always looks bad no matter what we do," "a chore to get my (fill in the blank) to mow it." The rest used the "pride" word.

When asked how they felt about their ornamental gardens, 78% responded extremely positively, with words like "therapeutic," "essential," "beautiful," and simply, "mine."

The women's response to the proposal of replacing their lawns with native plants met with little resistance: 17%. The most common concern was the expense and physical work anticipated. In fact, the majority of female respondents (82%) thought native replacements for their lawn would be "a good challenge," and a "wonderful idea!"

When asked about replacing their gardens with native plants, however, a whopping 87% responded "You leave my garden alone! "I like my garden the way it is!", sure that natives would be "drab," "dull," "too much work," and "too expensive!"

So what's going on in North America? Why this continuing obsession that sucks and pollutes our water supply (watering, fertilizing, applying pesticides), our time and energy (mowing and fertilizing), our clean air (mowing, leaf blowing), our peace and quiet (mowing, leaf blowing), not to mention our pocketbooks (all of the above)?

It's that old status thing: THESE are MY boundaries, and I have tamed nature! THIS IS MY TURF, literally. The obsession has taken root, from centuries of royal landscaping on the other side of the world, to yards in big and small towns across North America, and has damaged our environment in the process.

CHAPTER THREE

Go Eco, Go Biodiverse, Go Water-Friendly, Go Native!

What if the status symbol for the new millennium is NOT a lawn, but a beautiful yard full of ground covers, grasses, flowers, shrubs and trees that by their nature enhance our lives and help to keep the planet healthy?

DEFINITION OF "NATIVE"

A native, or indigenous, plant of North America is one which grew in a particular region of North America prior to European contact, i.e., it is native to that region.

DEFINITION OF "EXOTIC"

An exotic plant is one which was introduced into an area by design (man) or accident (wind, birds, flooding, etc.).

CAN YOU SAY "XER-I-SCAPE"?

When you xeriscape a yard, you plant specimens that once established need no water. These plants may be native or exotic.

Douglas Counter's front yard has been transformed from a sterile lawn into a native plant memorial garden. His lot is sunny and dry, so he planted prairie meadow flowers and grasses, using Ontario natives as well as some natives of the Great Plains Floristic Province. He never waters, unless establishing a new plant, and his sense of "status" is quite intact, thank you!
Douglas Counter photo

All About Native Plants: Adapt Or Die

Native plants have been evolving, without help or management from man, in their primal habitats for thousands, if not millions, of years. This evolution has made them hardy just where they are, in the conditions that are found where they are. It's been a kind of "adapt or die" scenario. So once properly established in the appropriate place in your yard (e.g., shade, sun, wet or dry, soil preference) they will need little care. No water after the first year. No fertilizers except mulches and compost. No pesticides.

Natives CAN Give You A Job Or Two

For those who are panicked at the thought of "nothing to do," don't worry, there are *some* "chores" associated with a native garden:

WATERING

Watering in the first year of a native plant's life in your garden is essential to allow the roots to grow into your soil. Water deeply and infrequently, to promote deep root growth. Each plant in each region of North America will have slightly different watering requirements their first year. You will need to do your homework and water accordingly. To make things easier and less wasteful, it is very important to group plants with similar water needs together in your garden.

COMPOSTING

For optimum native plant health, and as a brilliant environmental idea in its own right: COMPOST! Get yourself a sealed compost container with the little drawer in the bottom (available at your local hardware store), and put all non-meat and non-oil-based kitchen waste in it every day. Beautiful, crumbly dry compost will come out the bottom, and your plants will be thrilled when you spread it around them.

MULCHING

You can also gather up the leaves from your yard and neighbourhood that are going to the dump and use them as a nutritious mulch around your plants. Get some wood chips for mulch, too. Continual mulching will keep weeds down and provide a slow, constant source of food as it breaks down.

WEEDING

Some weeding will be necessary to keep the exotics and "weeds" out until the natives are established, and after that. Only weed by hand! The wonderful soil beasties, birds, butterflies, etc. that have come to your native garden will be harmed if you use chemical weed killers.

- - - - - - - - - - -

A WORD ABOUT THE GREAT NATIVE/XERISCAPE PLANT WARS

Some members of the school of xeriscape plant both natives and exotics, so long as they need little water. Some members of the school of native gardeners grow natives only, believing that reintroducing the natural habitat is as crucial as water conservation.

I don't have a true "side" in this debate.

I want to encourage North Americans to replace turf grass and exotic plants that need water, fertilizer and pesticides, primarily *because* they are not native, to restore the native ecosystem, as much as possible, *and* to reduce our criminal waste of water.

However, if you *must* plant a mix of natives and exotics, so be it. Just please make sure that they need no water, once established, and no chemicals for pest and disease control.

- - - - - - - - - - -

GROOMING

To get continuous bloom from your wildflowers, you will need to pick off old flower heads as they begin to fade and die. It's called dead-heading, and it greatly prolongs blooming time of native plants. You can prune shrubs and hedges to keep good air circulation around each plant in your yard. And if you must, there are natives that you can even mow...from once every few weeks, to once a year.

So you won't be bored, and suddenly without a job in the garden. Promise!

Talk To The Animals

As with flora, so with fauna. By reintroducing native plants to their original regions, you will begin to attract native wildlife back to your yard. Gorgeous butterflies, hummingbirds, song birds, birds that eat the insects that eat your plants, and even bumble-bees. If wildlife attraction is a part of going native for you, then check out what the food, shelter and water needs of the species you want to visit—and move in—are. You can create a veritable Garden of Eden of insect, bird and animal life! See Chapter Six for ideas.

Many Native Plant Choices

And your plants will be gorgeous! There are many diverse choices in the native plant families that offer a huge variety of colour and texture for each region of North America:

- flowering and fruit-bearing deciduous and evergreen trees
- evergreen, deciduous and flowering shrubs
- cacti, vines, flowers
- ground covers and grasses

There are drought lovers, swamp lovers, shade lovers, sun lovers, acidic and alkaline soil lovers, scented and unscented, tall, medium and low growers. Just look at the photos throughout this book; most of the plants in these yards are native to their regions and were planted according to their beauty and suitability to the site's conditions.

Shrubs provide natural fences and barriers, and shelter for animals. Fruit-bearing shrubs provide food and nesting sites for birds. In smaller gardens where shrubs would be overbearing, vines can be trailed over trellis and fence to provide privacy, shade, and a home and source of food (pollen, leaves, fruit, nectar) to birds.

Low-growing ground covers make great replacements for lawns in areas where you want to maintain a relatively flat surface. They hold the soil, preventing erosion—a good idea on slopes.

And flowers . . . well, native flowers are prolific in blooms, pollen and nectar, providing a beautiful view and essential food for the birds and the bees.

This carpet of stream-side violets (*Viola glabella*) is a beautiful alternative to a lawn in full or partial shade. The flowers are the exclusive hosts of a group of butterflies known as the "fritillaries." They include Aphrodite, Atlantis and silver bordered butterflies. Violets also attract the spring azure butterfly. *Eric Wold photo*

Native grasses in prairie and meadow habitats also prevent soil erosion, and will thrive in dry windy areas. And hey! If you can't do without that "lawn look," try buffalo grass in the appropriate region. You can mow it every two weeks or so with great results!

Native trees are an excellent consideration if you have the space, and are planting for the future. Make sure you take into account their full canopy spread as mature adults when deciding where to put them. Trees provide shelter and food for birds and small mammals and shade and beauty for humans, in all stages of their life cycles.

All This, And Economical, Too!

Let's talk money. Expense is a concern of many whose lawns and flower gardens are already established. But if you count up the financial and environmental costs of the annual plants, (see Myth 5, below), transformation does not seem so outrageous.

And it can be done a bit at a time.

Convinced? Curious? Read on!

Nine Common Myths About Using Native Plants

MYTH #1: Native plants produce pollens that are allergens, increasing hay fever in humans.
FACT: Conventional turf grass contains more allergenic pollens than native plants. Ditto ragweeds, which move into developed areas, and those showy, exotic flowers.

MYTH #2: Native plant gardens attract vermin and disease.
FACT: Vermin like garbage, not native plants. And native field mice like grains, not the type of native plants that will be used in your yard or garden. As for disease, the tick that carries Lyme disease occurs

in both native and exotic landscapes, and is carried by both wild and domestic animals.

MYTH #3: Native plants will become invasive in my garden and in other gardens in the neighbourhood.
FACT: They should be so lucky. Most, if not all plants considered "invasive" are exotics brought to this country from abroad, or to your neck of the woods from another part of North America.

MYTH #4: Native plant gardens will be drab and colourless.
FACT: There are fabulous, intensely bright and beautiful colours as well as reserved hues of bronze, silver, and copper represented in all the native plant communities of North America. Drop-dead gorgeous!

MYTH #5: Native plant gardens are too expensive.
FACT: Even though it will require some investment to switch to a native garden or yard, if you add up ALL the costs of maintaining a lawn or exotic garden including the cost of:

- water
- chemicals:
    - fertilizers
    - herbicides
    - insecticides
    - fungicides
    - lime
- mowers and mower maintenance
- gasoline and oil
- seed and seedlings
- sod and plugs
- annuals (those sales are killers!)
- dethatching
- aeration
- weeding

the initial investment of putting in a native garden bit by bit pales by comparison.

MYTH #6: Native plants are hard to grow, and too delicate. They don't last.

FACT: If you do your research properly and select plants that are native to your local region and that suit the conditions of your yard (shade, sun, moisture, etc.) the natives will THRIVE. They have been here for millennia. They are extremely hardy and strong.

MYTH #7: Native plants harbour mosquitoes.

FACT: Areas of standing water, not native plants, provide breeding grounds for mosquitoes.

MYTH #8: Native gardens look like "the bush": wild and messy.

FACT: Native gardens can look as sculptured and manicured as any formal, exotic garden or as wild as any meadow. The plant selection and design is up to you. Just check out the photo opposite. Does this look "messy" or "wild" to you?

MYTH #9: My municipality will only allow turf-grass lawns.

FACT: Most states and provinces in North America are actively encouraging residents to incorporate native plants into their yards and gardens a bit at a time to reduce dependence on water supplies. While some municipalities have yet to be converted and are giving native garden growers an opportunity to test the bylaws, others are learning, and even converting public spaces to native gardens.

The anything-but-dull, beautifully manicured yard at the home of the Romeros in Groene, Texas, is composed of both native and non-native plants. The lawn is buffalo grass (*Buchloe dactyloides*), which can be mowed like a turf-grass lawn. The plants in bloom include the pink flowered native shrub autumn sage (*Salvia greggii*) and the golden columbine (*Aquilegia chrysantha*); the touch of blue is courtesy of the Texas bluebonnet (*Lupinus texensis*). *Andy Wasowski photo*

CHAPTER FOUR

Eight Steps To Going Native

STEP ONE
Get Connected

The best way to learn about native plants is to meet others who have, or are, taking the plunge too. There are fantastic native plant societies and organizations that promote the use of and have education materials on native plants in North America (see resources section). These groups will provide the beginner with excellent advice and encouragement. Many have newsletters, regular meetings and garden tours. They also provide tips on the best nurseries and information sources in your area, as well as helpful hints on planting and caring for your natives.

Visit botanic gardens, arboreta and, with your native garden group, private gardens that have gone native. Visit nurseries that sell native plants, and begin a relationship.

And get out into the wild! Many native plant gardeners swear by nature's design (as opposed to "land-scaping") and try to faithfully re-create plant communities from the wild in their own yards. Visit a nearby meadow, state or national park. There's nothing like the wild to discover what colours and shapes go together naturally.

And read, read, read. There are fabulous books available on native plant gardening for every region in North America (see "Further Reading").

● ● ● ● ● ● ● ● ● ● ● ●
WALKABOUT ETIQUETTE

When on your walk, be sure to tread carefully and lightly, so as not to damage any wild flora or fauna. **And never remove plants from the wild!**

Take pictures, not plants!
● ● ● ● ● ● ● ● ● ● ● ●

STEP TWO
Get And Keep Your Neighbours On-Board

Some people are very fearful and suspicious of nature, and by association, native gardens. Here are a few ideas to defuse the fear and anger:

Talk to your neighbours before you even pull up that first rectangle of turf. Let them know what you are planning, and why. Same with the local officials. Educate those around you about the good ecological sense of your project, and chances are, they'll be curious, and even make the switch themselves.

Start small (see step three, below) for your own sake, as well as those around you. If done in small portions, gradually, neighbours will have a chance to become acclimatized to the change.

Consider putting a border around your yard. A low fence made out of natural

Adrian van Veenendaal puts the finishing touches on his family's newly planted butterfly garden at their home in Ladner, British Columbia, in May 1997. Signage like this can go a long way towards softening community relations. To see how this garden grew, see page 60. *Edward van Veenendaal photo*

materials (split rail, for example), or a native hedge, can go a long way to diminish conflict.

Proudly put a sign up. It's hard for people to be fearful of a "butterfly garden."

Use paths covered in mulch, bird-baths, clearings covered in ground covers, bird feeders, sundials and a sitting area with a bench to humanize your yard. Not only will it be more "user friendly" to you, your family and friends, it will reassure neighbours that you are not trying to re-create the wild, but purposefully and beautifully designing a garden using native plants.

And finally, allow your neighbours to have their own opinions. Don't fall into the trap of becoming a self-appointed preacher, attempting to convert others to native gardening. It doesn't work. If neighbours see a gorgeous native garden, they may be tempted to start asking questions about it. If they remain hostile and wedded to their rider mowers and shaved lawns, so be it.

STEP THREE
How Much Is Enough?

Your first decision in planning your transition to native landscaping is to determine how much of your yard(s) to transform in the first year. My recommendation is to start small—very small—so that your initiation will be an easy and pleasant one.

There are a few issues to consider:

- How much physical labour do you want to do or pay to have done this fall?
- How much money is in the budget for this year's portion of the project?

- How much time do you have to invest in the project this growing year?

Restoration can take place beautifully a bit at a time, and if you go slowly, you'll be giving yourself the time needed to learn about this new way of gardening.

To start: choose an area that will need the least amount of physical labour and expense. For example, transforming a small (two-metre square or five-foot square) section of lawn makes more sense than replacing a few nine-metre (thirty-foot) non-native trees and large shrubs in your first year.

Be thinking about these factors as you follow the next steps in your planning.

STEP FOUR
Get To Know Your Grounds!

As you begin to attend native plant society meetings, visit arboreta, walk the woods, prairies and meadows in your region looking for ideas, it is essential that you get to know YOUR site, intimately.

To start, walk your yard, and either mentally or physically map all the permanent features, such as the buildings, decks, paved areas, fences and walls. Some folks support the no-map, no-formal-design approach to native gardening, striving instead to re-create nature's design as much as possible in plant selection and placement. Others would be lost without graph paper and overlays. As you walk your property, decide which method works best for you.

If you go for the more formal approach, map, on a large piece of paper, as much to scale as possible, all the buildings, driveways, sidewalks and pathways, as well as:

- the play areas;
- the organic vegetable garden (the only yard component I believe should legally be allowed consistent water!);
- the compost pile;

- high/medium/low foot traffic areas;
- the views you want blocked;
- the views to be opened;
- the areas to be planted in tall plants and trees;
- the areas to be planted in medium height plants;
- the areas to be planted in low-growing plants;
- the areas to be planted in ground covers; and
- fences/walls you want to cover with foliage.

This is your Structural Map. Attach it to a wooden or plastic drawing board. Cardboard will most likely not be sturdy enough, especially for the next part of this step. Over the next weeks or months, in rain and shine, in morning, at high noon, and midafternoon, begin to observe and again mark mentally or physically on a piece of tracing paper taped over the structural map, the following:

- north, south, east, and west;
- where water puddles;
- where water drains quickly;
- slopes and indentations;
- completely and partially sunny areas early, midday, and midafternoon;
- partially or completely shady areas early, midday, and midafternoon;
- where snow/frost lingers in winter;
- areas of sandy soil;
- areas of hardpan soil;
- areas of loamy soil.
- areas of clay soil;
- the pH of the soil in the open and under trees;
- the direction of the prevailing winds;
- the maximum and minimum annual temperatures in the yard; and

- the amount of rain on the yard in spring, summer, fall, and winter.

This will be your mental or physical Environmental Overlay.

STEP FIVE
Can You Say "Flor-is-tic Province"?

Now that you have begun to get to know your yard as never before, it's time to place it in the larger scheme of things. North America can be divided into several regions based on native plant distribution and climate patterns. These regions are called "Floristic Provinces." Keep in mind, however, that within these, and often, *within your own yard*, are many bioregions and specific site conditions that will further determine what kind of plants will do well in which areas.

Various sources delineate the regions in slightly different ways, but for the purposes of this book, we'll use the following:

1 The California Floristic Province
2 The Pacific Northwest
3 The Western Mountains and Basins
4 The Southwestern Deserts
5 The Great Plains
6 The Eastern Woodlands
7 The Coastal Plains

Each Floristic Province has its own distinct characteristics, and exquisitely beautiful native plants that are well adapted to the home garden.

It is important to use plants native to the Floristic Province and immediate bioregion that your property is in to ensure survival of that plant with the least amount of input and environmental disruptions.

A gorgeous California Floristic Province yard, planted at the Santa Barbara Botanic Garden, California, using natives to the area. The lawn is blue grama grass (*Bouteloua gracilis*), the yellow-flowered shrub is "Pacific Sunset," a hybrid of two native Fremontias (*Fremontodendron* spp.) and the blue-flowered shrub in the foreground is a Ceanothus hybrid (*Ceanothus* spp.). The border of silver shrubbery is saffron buckwheat (*Eriogonum crocatum*). *Andy Wasowski photo*

Okay, you may ask, what's the difference between the climate zone maps that NORMAL gardeners use and a map of the Floristic Provinces? Which one is best for figuring out which native plants will do well in my yard?

A climate zone, or plant hardiness zone map will give you, in great detail, temperature highs and lows of a region delineated by a circle. There are zones within zones, depending on elevation, proximity of water, etc. The Floristic Provinces Map shows the natural ranges of native plants in broad strokes. The best idea is to use both as basic guidelines: determine the temperature extremes of your immediate area, and the natives of your Floristic Province that will suit the conditions of your yard.

A Pacific Northwest native yard in Roberts Creek, British Columbia, covered in velvety native mosses and salal (*Gaultheria shallon*). In late spring, the salal will bear beautiful clusters of pinkish flowers shaped like drooping goblets. The delicately flavoured fruit, a historical favourite of first peoples, is now widely enjoyed on its own or in preserves.
Kai Goodwin photo

Each Floristic Province is described in Chapter Seven, along with a list of "easy to grow" natives for each province.

The view from the front porch of Lloyd Davies' home in Vernon, BC, shows natives and non-natives in his "xeriscape" garden. The Western Mountain and Basins native plants include phlox (*Phlox douglasii*), yarrow (*Achillea* spp.), penstemons (*Penstemon* spp.) and western blue flag (*Iris missouriensis*). The lovely pink flowering phlox at the centre of the photograph is a Wenatchee native, *Leptodactylon pungens*. Lloyd practices true xeriscaping; the yard is never watered, except around a new seedling. *Janet Armstrong photo*

From the front cover, a stunning example of native landscaping in the Southwestern Deserts Floristic Province. This yard in Las Vegas, Nevada, includes Joshua trees (*Yucca brevifolia*), gold California poppies (*Eschscholzia californica*), the red Parry's penstemon (*Penstemon parryi*) and other native cacti, shrubs, flowers and ground covers. *Andy Wasowski photo*

The native prairie garden at the Forks Historic Site, Winnipeg, Manitoba, Canada, installed and maintained by Shirley Froehlich, of Prairie Originals, St. Andrews, Manitoba, includes Great Plains Floristic Province plants fringed sage (*Artemisia frigida*), wild bergamot (*Monarda fistulosa*), and Indian grass (*Sorghastrum nutans*). *Shirley Froehlich photo*

The Eastern Woodlands Floristic Province is beautifully represented at the Quaker Hill Native Plant Garden in Pawling, New York. This scene, from their "Rich Cove Forest" shows (foreground) cardinal flowers (*Lobelia cardinalis*), summersweet (*Clethra alnifolia*) and marginal wood fern (*Dryopteris marginalis*). The groundcover between the cracks in the path is creeping phlox (*Phlox stolonifera*).
Quaker Hill Native Plant Garden photo

Some of the lush native plants of the Coastal Plains Floristic Province in the Steward garden in Pointe Coupee Parish, Louisiana, are, left to right: a native tree, beargrass (*Yucca flaccida*) and a clump of purple coneflowers (*Echinacea purpurea*). Coral , or trumpet, honeysuckle (*Lonicera sempervirens*) has flung itself over the gate, reaching for the sunlight. *Andy Wasowski photo*

North American Floristic Provinces Map

This map shows the regions, or Floristic Provinces, of distribution patterns of native plants according to climatic and other conditions. Each plant listed in Chapter Seven will have a natural range within its Floristic Province and may not cover the entire area.

California Floristic Province
The Pacific Northwest
The Western Mountains and Basins
The Southwestern Deserts
The Great Plains
The Eastern Woodlands
The Coastal Plains

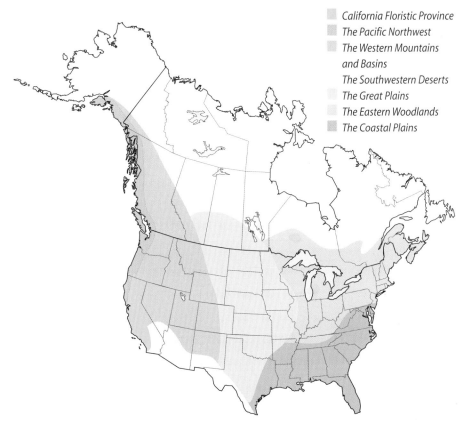

Climate Zones

The United States Department of Agriculture produces a North American Climate Zone Map which provides climate extremes throughout North America. Each plant listing given in Chapter Seven of this book includes Zone designations. Check with your local nursery to determine the zone of your garden.

1	*below -50°F*
2	*-50° to -40°F*
3	*-40° to -30°F*
4	*-30° to -20°F*
5	*-20° to -10°F*
6	*-10° to 0°F*
7	*0° to 10°F*
8	*10° to 20°F*
9	*20° to 30°F*
10	*30° to 40°F*
11	*above 40°F*

STEP SIX

Ladies And Gentlemen, Start Your Lists!

As you familiarize yourself with the characteristics of your Floristic Province, and as you begin to visit reputable nurseries, local native plant society meetings, botanic gardens, arboreta, and the bookstore or library, refer to your environmental map, and begin to jot down names of plants that are native to your area and that suit that spot you have in mind in your yard. A good place to start is with the lists of "easy-to-grow" natives in Chapter Seven.

One thing to remember when you are plotting your natives on your map: plants that need the same water requirements are best grouped together to make first-year watering easier and less wasteful.

As mentioned earlier, many "non-designer" native gardeners use the walkabout method to give them ideas for their gardens, hoping to more accurately re-create what occurs, rather than plotting a map, and filling in the spaces. If that suits you, go for it! If not, design, by all means.

Wherever you fall in love with native plants, begin to write down their names, if available, and add a written description, and photograph, if possible, so that you can identify the plants and research their needs.

If you need to establish names of plants, you can look in one of the many regional native plant books published for your area or take photos to your local Native Plant Society meeting, botanic garden, arboretum, or nursery. Tips on ensuring you are shopping at an ethical nursery follow in Chapter Five.

Some nurseries are "getting with the program" and are learning about and stocking native plants these days (see resources section). If yours aren't, encourage them by telling them you'll spend your garden dollars at their store when they stock the natives you need.

STEP SEVEN

Research And Refine

As you interact with other native gardeners at meetings, on-line, through reading and at nurseries, begin to narrow down your list of possibilities through extensive research on each plant you are considering.

Is the plant native to my immediate bioregion? Is it available at a reputable nursery in seed, bulb, plug, or seedling? What is the blooming time? Will it do well in that sunny/shady/cool/hot/wet/dry part of the garden? Will it do well in that high traffic area I have in mind?

Cross off your list any plants that do not meet these basic requirements, and start looking for other plants that do.

Now you are ready to double check each plant species' placement. Singles or groupings, make sure you place the plant where its requirements for a thriving life will be met!

Or, to put it another way, the most important thing to remember when choosing and placing native plants in the garden is to *let the plants tell you where they need to go.* This will spare you countless hours of trying to revive a sickly plant that really needed to be in, say, partial shade instead of full sun, and countless dollars in replacements.

If you are the mapping kind, draw circles that represent plant groupings on another overlay of tracing paper, and write the names of the plants that will go in the grouping inside each circle. This will be your "Plant Map."

Now you are ready to prepare the garden bed!

STEP EIGHT

Out With The Old!

If you are starting your native gardening career on an established lawn, you can rent a sod cutter that runs like a Rototiller for large areas, or use a garden edger for small areas.

Top left: The front yard of Eric Wold and Brinda Narayan-Wold as it looked before the start of their native gardening project. Boring. Could be anywhere, uses hundreds of gallons of water each year to keep it green. *Eric Wold photo*

Bottom left: Brinda Narayan-Wold grins as she removes turf from the front of her home in Eugene, Oregon, in preparation for planting a native yard. *Eric Wold photo*

Below: The same yard after the project has begun. Eric is preparing the "hard scape" for the front yard, which will be covered in a mulch of bark and soil and planted with over twenty species native to the Willamette Valley. The two-foot wall is made of Coburg basalt, a rock type local to the Eugene area. *Brinda Narayan-Wold photo*

Top right: The front yard as it looked before Douglas Counter started his native plant memorial garden at his Toronto home.

Bottom right: July, 1999. The front yard, now a memorial garden, was planted in native & non-native wildflowers in July, 1997. Douglas has just put seedlings in the ditch in front of the sidewalk.

Below: July, 2001, and the front and ditch gardens are a delight! Even when neighbouring yards turn brown in drought despite consuming hundreds of gallons of water, this little bit of prairie looks magnificent without a drop.

Species in the front garden include purple coneflower (*Echinacea purpurea*), wild bergamot (*Monarda fistulosa*), Canada wild rye (*Elymus canadensis*), spotted Joe Pye weed (*Eupatorium maculatum*) and big bluestem grass (*Andropogon gerardii*).

Species in the ditch garden include butterfly milkweed (*Asclepias tuberosa*), little bluestem grass (*Schizachyrium scoparium*), hairy beardtongue (*Penstemon hirsutus*), foxtail sedge (*Carex vulpinoides*), and sideoats grama (*Bouteloua curtipendula*).

Top left: The side garden at Douglas Counter's residence before his native plant memorial garden project.

Bottom left: July, 1998. The side garden after native plants have been "in" one season.

Below: July, 1999. The side garden in a more mature state.

Species include Canada goldenrod (*Solidago canadensis*), wild bergamot (*Monarda fistulosa*), purple coneflower (*Echinacea purpurea*), black-eyed Susan (*Rudbeckia hirta*) and spotted Joe Pye weed (*Eupatorium maculatum*).

Then it's simply a matter of slicing the sod and soil to a depth of 20 centimetres (8 inches) into pieces or strips, and removing the grass plants and roots. Some people have found it easier to water first, or wait for a rainfall, let the lawn partially dry, then cut and remove the plants. The roots will come out of the soil more easily when moist. Rake the soil to remove any root material over the next few days. The more you get now, the less you'll have to "weed" out later!

If you are starting your native garden on a site that now contains exotic plants, dig them up carefully, getting all the roots, and have a sale!

This method may seem labour intensive (told you to start small!) but if you are thinking of using a Rototiller to turn the turf/existing garden under, think again! You will be digging under not only the roots, but also millions of seeds from your weeds, lawn and garden plants, which will sprout and fight with your native plants for years to come.

Another approach is to smother the existing plants, rather than dig them up. This can be done by covering them with thick sheets of black plastic for one growing season. If you don't want to wait a year, and have the budget, you can also smother those unwanted plants by placing thick layers (10 thicknesses, minimum) of newspaper, or 30 centimetres (12 inches) of leaves over the existing area, then buying soil and shovelling it on top of the paper to the depth required by your new natives.

Some native plants require little soil, others many inches, as you'll discover in your educational journey.

When all roots of the former plants are gone, and the soil is completely clean, you will be ready to plant!

CHAPTER FIVE

In With The New

How To Shop For Native Plants And An Ethical Nursery

Selecting an appropriate source for your native plants is an important step. Once again, *do not get your plants or cuttings from the wild.* There are nurseries, native plant societies, botanic gardens, arboreta and other gardeners that can supply you with information, seeds, and plants. In fact, in most areas in North America, it is actually illegal to poach natives.

There is a reason for this. You are helping to return a vanishing part of our native habitat by growing a native garden. *Don't be part of its destruction to do so.*

At The Nursery

Here are some excellent and essential questions to ask when you are shopping for native plants at a nursery:

1 Is this species native to our local area, within our Floristic Province?

There is a large range in what nurseries and their suppliers call "native." Beware! Sometimes it is called "native" because it is native to North America, but not your region. If it's not native to your region, move on, shopper!

Sometimes, you'll see a plant being sold as "native" further north/south/east/west than its truly native habitat. It could be a genetically modified plant that makes it more hardy/rain tolerant/drought tolerant, etc. This is a cultivar, which is another way of saying it was manufactured to pretend to be a native. NOT!

Sometimes the species you are looking at is native to your region, but that particular *variety* is not. Check it out; give preference to local varieties that were locally produced when buying native plants.

The North American Native Plant Society has a list of ethical guidelines for gardeners. They believe that regardless of where you live and garden, you can ensure that your activities do not harm native plant communities in the wild by following these rules:

1   Do not disrupt native plant communities.

2   Obtain native plants from seed, garden, or nursery.

3   Buy only wildflowers, ferns and cacti certified by the vendors as "nursery propagated."

4   Use plants and seeds that have originated in your immediate bioregion. Such plants and seeds are best adapted to the local climate, soil, predators, pollinators and disease.

5   Give preference to bioregionally native plant species in your garden, rather than naturalized or exotic species. The latter group may escape to wild habitats and interfere with the growth and spread of native flora and fauna.

6   Promote the cultivation and propagation of bioregionally native plants as an educational and conservation measure to supplement the preservation of natural habitat.

7   Keep accurate records of any bioregionally rare flora which you are growing to increase our understanding of the biology of the species.

8   Transplant native flora only when the plants of a given area are officially slated for

destruction (e.g., road construction, subdivisions, pipelines, golf courses, etc.). Obtain permission before transplanting.

9   Collect no more than 10% of a seed crop from the wild. Leave the rest for natural dispersal and as food for dependent organisms.

10 Use natural means of fertilizing, weed and predator control rather than synthetic chemicals.

11 Consider planting native species to attract native fauna, especially birds, butterflies, and moths uncommon to your bioregion.

12 Exercise extreme caution when studying and photographing wildflowers in order not to damage the surrounding flora and fauna.

13 Co-operate with institutions like arboreta, botanical gardens, museums and universities in the propagation and study of rare species.

14 Openly share your botanic knowledge with the public, but ensure that native plant species or communities will not be damaged in the process.

(with permission of the North American Native Plant Society, Toronto, Ontario, Canada)

2 What is the source of the plant I am holding in my hand?

If a supplier doesn't know or is extremely vague in their answer, shop at another nursery. Collecting from the wild is disappearing, but some nurseries and suppliers still do it. Take the effort to find one that is ethical.

3 Are these salvaged plants? If so, where were they salvaged? Did you get a permit for salvage?

Plant collection in an area slated for destruction/construction is fine, but permits are issued in most states and provinces now. Again, ask your nursery if they received such a permit.

4 Where are your seed sources?

Seeds should be collected as close to the planting site as possible. If seeds were sold to the nursery by a supplier, make sure the nursery knows where the seeds came from.

It's important that your source of native plants is knowledgeable and reputable. Seed crop rows of little bluestem (*Schizachyrium scoparium*) at Mary Gartshore's Pterophylla Native Plants & Seeds, Walsingham, Ontario.
Mary Gartshore photo

5 Were the seeds collected appropriately?

Seed collection is fine, as long as not more than 10% of that year's seed has been collected. To take more diminishes the chances of that plant continuing to reseed.

6 Is this plant on an endangered, threatened or special concern list?

If the answer is yes, don't buy it. They are illegally selling plants.

The answers to these questions are important!

We protect a species by preserving the genetic variation contained in local varieties. Not only will planting a non-local variety dilute the local native variety, but these non-local plants are just not going to grow as well as plants that were raised from local stock. Each local variety of a species with a wide geographical distribution has spent many thousands of years adapting to the particularities of its local conditions.

Many nurseries around the continent are just beginning to stock native plants. Many buy what their suppliers send, period. You can help these nurseries to become more ethically and environmentally aware by asking these questions, letting them know the correct responses, and encouraging them with your choice to shop with them if they receive and sell natives in an ethical manner.

Take a part in ethical reintroduction of native species to your area with the power and persuasion of your shopping dollars!

CHAPTER SIX

Specialty Gardens

A Word About Wildlife

The first step to planning a garden for wildlife is to determine which plants, shrubs, and trees will provide food, shelter and water for the species you want to attract. The reverse is true, as well. If you find unwanted wildlife in your yard, determine what is attracting it (e.g., bears to Kinnikinnick are like bees to honey) and remove the temptation.

As always, for your native plants to thrive, first and foremost, you have to place them where the conditions of your yard suit them best. So if there's one particular plant that attracts the one particular butterfly you want as a visitor, and that plant needs shade, please don't try to make it survive in your sunny yard. It won't work. The plant will die, and the butterfly will go elsewhere anyway.

Ditto for planting a woodland garden. If you don't have, or plan to create sufficient shade for those woodland dwellers, give up the idea, and go for a sunny meadow planting instead.

Remember, let the plants tell you where they need to go. And if that means not in your yard, so be it!

How To Grow A Butterfly Garden

Butterflies are attracted to brightly coloured native flowers that produce nectar for food. These can be

BUTTERFLY GARDEN in progress

Remember the picture of the young boy hammering the "Butterfly Garden" sign on page 35? Here is the garden in Ladner, British Columbia, Canada, in August of the same summer. Plants include black-eyed Susans (Rudbeckia hirta), Verbena (Verbena bonariensis) and blue-pod Lupines (Lupinus polyphyllus). Edward van Veenendaal photo

on trees, shrubs, wildflowers, and ground covers. Butterflies will look for choice leaves to lay their eggs, using scent and taste organs to determine the best bet.

If it's a butterfly garden you want, check out your region in the section on your Floristic Province, in Chapter Seven, and with your local library, nursery and Native Plant society to determine which plants to put in your yard to attract local butterflies, or those on their migrating pattern.

Some of the plants on the "easy-to-grow" lists found in Chapter Seven that attract butterflies are:

Aster	Bush Dalea
Azalea	Cardinal Flower
Bee Balm	Carolina Jessamine
Big Bluestem	Chokecherry
Blanket Flower	Chuparosa
Blue Elderberry	Claretcup Cactus
Bluebell	Columbine
Brittlebrush	Daisies
Brodiaea	Desert Marigold
Buckeye	Desert Willow

Dogwood
Downy Hawthorn
Eastern Cottonwood
Eastern Red Cedar
Eastern Redbud
Fairyduster
Flowering Currants
Green-and-gold
Honey Mesquite
Hydrangea
Iris
Joshua Tree
Lilac
Lily
Lupine
Magnolia
Manzanita
Nootka Rose
Ocotillo

Palo Verde
Paper Birch
Penstemon
Phlox
Purple Coneflower
Rabbitbrush
Rose Verbena
Sage
Saskatoon Serviceberry
Sassafras
Scarlet Monkey-flower
Silverbell
Summersweet
Sundrops
Toyon
Trumpet Honeysuckle
Violet
Wild Onion

Planning And Planting A Bird Garden

The first thing to determine when planning a bird garden is which local birds you want to attract. Go to your library and take out a book on birds that nest or rest in your area. Make a list of the ones you like and their feeding requirements. Then take a look at the plants listed below, and note any that attract those birds. Be sure *you* like the plants, too! Note their requirements for water, sun, soil, etc., in Chapter Seven, and match them with a site in your yard.

1 Feed Them
Year-round food is an important factor. This means selecting plants with an eye for keeping the dinner plate full all year with fruits, berries, seeds and insects.

It may also mean supplementing food with store-bought seed, suet and fruit.

Sue and Ed Mahoney's woodland backyard garden in Springfield, Illinois, is land-scaped exclusively as a bird habitat, and includes native Easter lilies (*Lilium longiflorum*), Virginia bluebell (*Mertensia virginica*), wild columbine (*Aquilegia canadensis*), purple cone-flowers (*Echinacea purpurea*), Virginia creeper (*Parthenocissus quinquefolia*), bleeding heart (*Dicentra eximia*), trumpet vine (*Bignonia capreolata*), hemlock (*Tsuga canadensis*) and eastern white pine (*Pinus strobus*). *Chris Young photo*

2 Give Them Shelter

Second on the importance list for birds is shelter. Evergreen shrubs or trees provide the best cover for birds, but if your yard is too small for these, anything that provides shelter will do: deciduous plants and shrubs, stone walls, old hollow trees, etc. Build nesting boxes for nesting families if you don't have large shrubs or trees. It's a great project to involve the kids in.

When situating the boxes, be sure to take local felines and racoons into account. It may be necessary to construct a raccoon guard around the box to dissuade chick poaching.

3 Water Your Birds

Water is also essential to attracting and keeping birds in your yard. A shallow birdbath, kept clean and full from collected rainwater is all you need. Place the bath on a high pedestal in the open if there are cats about. Put a washed rock in it for a perch, and set it in a sunny place.

Birdbaths can be made out of a variety of materials, from ceramic dishes to hollow log halves. Store-bought fibreglass models also work.

Below is a list of plants from the "easy-to-grow" sections of Chapter Seven, listed by Floristic Province, and the birds they attract:

CALIFORNIA FLORISTIC PROVINCE

California Fuchsia	hummingbirds
Douglas Iris	hummingbirds
Leopard Lily	hummingbirds
Foothill Penstemon	hummingbirds
Toyon (Holly)	warblers, thrashers, starlings, towhees, sparrows
California Buckeye	yellow-billed cuckoo, downy woodpeckers

PACIFIC NORTHWEST FLORISTIC PROVINCE

Kinnikinnick	California thrashers, rufous-sided towhees, fox sparrows
Red Columbine	hummingbirds
Leopard Lily	hummingbirds
Pacific Rhodos	hummingbirds
Salal	thrashers, towhees, sparrows, also bears and deer!
Nootka Rose	hummingbirds
Pink-Flowering Currant	hummingbirds, warblers, thrashers, sparrows, etc.
Holly-Leaf Cherry	finches, thrashers, sparrows

**WESTERN MOUNTAINS
AND BASINS FLORISTIC PROVINCE**

Western Blue Flag	hummingbirds
Mosquito Plant	hummingbirds
Indian Pink	hummingbirds

Creeping Mahonia	fruit-eating birds
Sideoats Grama	meadowlarks
Datil	nesting birds
Beardlip Penstemon	hummingbirds
Rabbitbrush	finches, pine siskins
Golden Currant	hummingbirds, fruit eaters
Sask. Serviceberry	fruit-eating birds
Quaking Aspen	red-naped sapsucker, owls, swallows, bluebirds
Pinyon Pine	pinyon jay, quail, Stellar's jay

SOUTHWESTERN DESERTS FLORISTIC PROVINCE

Claretcup Cactus	hummingbirds, orioles, songbirds, doves
Desert Marigold	seed-eating birds
Yellow Columbine	hummingbirds
Dorri Sage	hummingbirds
Pink Fairy Duster	bobwhites, quail
Cholla	cactus wrens, road runners
Brittlebrush	songbirds
Chuparosa	hummingbirds, warblers, orioles, goldfinches
Joshua Tree	woodpeckers, doves, songbirds, flickers
Blue Palo Verde	doves
Ocotillo	orioles, songbirds, hummingbirds
Desert Willow	pigeons, doves, hummingbirds
Honey Mesquite	nesting birds

THE GREAT PLAINS FLORISTIC PROVINCE

Blue Grama	wild turkeys, finches, longspurs
Little Bluestem	meadowlarks, finches, juncos, sparrows
Buffalo Grass	songbirds, sparrows, juncos

Indian Grass	songbirds, finches
Purple Coneflower	goldfinch, seed eaters
Blue Sage	hummingbirds
Cardinal Flower	hummingbirds
Chokecherry	kingbird, robin, fruit eaters
Downy Hawthorn	towhees, sparrows, cedar waxwings
Eastern Cottonwood	orioles, grosbeaks
Trumpet Creeper	hummingbirds

THE EASTERN WOODLANDS FLORISTIC PROVINCE

Wild Columbine	hummingbirds
Dwarf Iris	hummingbirds
Carolina Phlox	hummingbirds
Bee Balm	hummingbirds
Sundrops	hummingbirds
Bearberry	grouse, songbirds
Eastern Redbud	blue jays, nesting birds
Sassafras	kingbird, phoebe, catbirds, pileated woodpecker
Red-Osier Dogwood	wood ducks, grosbeaks, robins, thrushes, cedar waxwings
Paper Birch	pine siskin, redpoll, seed eaters

THE COASTAL PLAINS FLORISTIC PROVINCE

Crested Iris	hummingbirds
Virginia Bluebell	hummingbirds
Honeysuckle	hummingbirds, cardinals, catbirds
Carolina Jessamine	hummingbirds
Flowering Dogwood	bluebird, bobwhites, mockingbirds, robins, quail, etc.
Sour Gum Tree	bobwhites, buntings, finches, flickers, grosbeaks, etc.

How To Grow
A Woodland Garden

The most obvious requirement for a woodland garden is sufficient shade for your plants. So, as with all other native gardening projects, the first step is to observe your site as it is, and note sun and shade patterns at different times of the day before you buy and plant. Some woodland plants do well in morning sun for a few hours, but will die in the intense heat and sun of midafternoon. So document the sun, water, soil and shade patterns well on your planning map, and begin to make a list of desired plants according to their requirements.

Get out into woodland areas in your neighbourhood to observe plant communities, and how combinations of various species seem to go together.

If the woodland plants you want to grow require more moisture and/or shade than your yard delivers, you have at least two choices:

1 Plant for the future. This means putting in a few "early succession" species of trees, shrubs or ground covers that will grow and fill in quickly, providing shade in a year to three years. Follow this up by planting "climax" trees that will take much longer to mature and provide shade for decades to come.

2 If you can't wait for the above, change your plans and plant a sunnier meadow garden.

If you are gardening on an already wooded site, remove the non-native trees and shrubs that require watering, and replace them with natives.

Taking the lower limbs off trees provides open shade, with room underneath for wildflower plantings, or a quiet spot for contemplative sitting.

The wooded stream garden at Quaker Hill Native Plant Garden in Pawling, New York, boasts natives that like cool shade and wet feet, including (left to right) swamp rose mallow (*Hibiscus moscheutos*), swamp milkweed (*Asclepias incarnata*), as well as sweet Joe Pye weed (*Eupatorium purpureum*), summersweet (*Clethra alnifolia*) in bloom with white flowers, and a cinnamon fern (*Osmunda cinnamomea*). The trees, left to right, are eastern red cedar (*Juniperus virginiana*), red buckeye (*Aesculus pavia*), and American holly (*Ilex opaca*). *Quaker Hill Native Plant Garden photo*

Use pathways covered in gravel or chip mulch to lead to particular viewpoints, or just to make an interesting walkway.

Maintenance in the first year for your plants will mean watering until the roots have established themselves. Water deeply, and infrequently to promote deep root growth. You will also have to weed to remove "undesirables" from time to time.

Top: Mary Stamp of Milwaukee, Wisconsin, has planted a woodland garden that is 95% native to her area in trees, shrubs, ground covers and ferns. A bird's delight! *Andy Wasowski photo*

Bottom: If you live in the Eastern Woodlands Floristic province but do not have shade, you can either plant shade trees and wait, or, as Douglas Counter has done in Toronto, plant a meadow garden. *Douglas Counter photo*

In the fall, the woodland garden mulches itself with fallen leaves. The most natural thing to do is let them slowly decompose and feed your plants.

How To Grow A Meadow Or Wildflower Garden

Meadow gardens do best in the Western Mountains and Basins, and the Great Plains regions. Elsewhere, they will need monitoring and weeding of species that are trying to take the meadow over and revert it to woodlands. That doesn't mean you can't grow a meadow in the other regions, just that a higher maintenance regime of weeding and mowing will be needed to freeze your garden in time.

Preparation for a meadow is the same as for all other native gardens: the existing species should be removed by digging or smothering and adding topsoil. Meadows like an occasional mow (every year or so) to keep the plants strong. You won't need heavy fertilizers, just organic mulch and/or compost.

Unlike woodland gardens, meadow and wildflower gardens need plenty of sunlight. So make sure you have an area that gets five hours of sunlight a day. There are many different easy ways to go about creating a meadow, but one important note: those meadows-in-a-can and wildflowers-in-a-can are not the way to go. Avoid them!

Meadows aren't THAT easy, and the cans, which seem to offer a vast garden of gorgeous bright colour, do not a meadow make. Most have non-natives, as well as annuals in their mix, which will die off quickly. Get some good advice and perennial seeds at a reputable nursery instead, and you'll have a long-lasting meadow of different textures, colours and species.

Meadows are a mixture of plants. In fact, you'll need at least two dozen different local species in your mix that are suited to your yard, to have a successful, long-lasting meadow garden.

Mary Gartshore, of Pterophylla Native Plants & Seeds in Walsingham, Ontario, has a gorgeous prairie yard that shows mostly Butterfly milkweed (*Asclepias tuberosa*), but it also includes other dry prairie species in a blend that emulates regional natural sites.
Mary Gartshore photo

The other maintenance chore required is mowing the meadow at the end of the second year, sometime after the seeds have ripened. Set the newly sharpened blades at the highest setting. After that, mow every year, once a year.

Here is an example of the number and kinds of species necessary for a successful prairie meadow, courtesy of *The Wild Ones Natural Landscapers Handbook*:

- 2–3 nurse species (annual flax, annual rye, oats, winter wheat)
- 2–6 pioneers, wild rye, black-eyed Susan, evening primrose

Another prairie wildflower garden, this time on the Lamb property in Kitchener, Ontario, Canada; this one shows a perennial border of black-eyed Susans (*Rudbeckia hirta*), raspberry coloured wild bergamot (*Monarda fistulosa*) and the bright purplish-blue petals of Ohio spiderwort (*Tradescantia ohiensis*). *Andy Wasowski photo*

- 6–10 early succession forbs or grasses: yellow prairie coneflower, bee balm, New England aster, thimbleweed and
- 20–30 site specific grasses and forbs

The Wild Ones Natural Landscapers, Ltd. in Milwaukee, have local chapters throughout the Prairies (www.for-wild.com) and are an amazing group of people, dedicated to getting the word out to those planting natives. Their *The Wild Ones Natural Landscapers Handbook* is available for free on-line.

CHAPTER SEVEN

The Floristic Provinces

This is a basic introduction to the natural native plant ranges in North America called Floristic Provinces. The Floristic Provinces North-America-wide map is on page 48. Each of the provinces listed below is illustrated with its own map showing the states and provinces it contains.

Each Floristic Province begins with a brief geographical description. Next comes a general description of the climate, followed by the region's plant history, and plant quirks, if any. Next, under "Site Preparation" come hints on soil preparation/landscaping needed for the plants to feel at home. Finally, there is a small list of classic, available and relatively easy-to-grow natives in three categories: Low: under 60 cm (24 in); Medium: 60–180 cm (2–6 ft); and Tall: 180 cm (6 ft) and over.

The plant listings start with the plant's common name, followed in brackets by the genus and species name. The second line lists any other common names. The third line lists the climatic zones and height range of the plant, followed by a brief description of the foliage and flowers, a note on whether the plant is perennial or annual, deciduous or evergreen. Next come the plant's sun and water requirements, followed in the next line by the soil requirements and how best to propagate. The next line lists some of the insects, birds, and mammals that the plant attracts. Special notes of interest, if any, are listed on the last line.

EXAMPLE

Wild Bergamot (*Monarda fistulosa*)	common name, genus and species
a.k.a. bee balm, oregano, Oswego tea	other common names
Zones 3–9. 60–90 cm (2–3 ft)	climate zone(s), plant height
Upright square stems, clusters of fragrant purple flowers	plant description
Perennial	perennial /annual/ evergreen
Full sun–partial shade, moderate water	sun and water requirements
All soils except dry; from seed, seedlings	preferred soils & propagation
Attracts butterflies, hummingbirds, bees	what it attracts
Edible as an herb	notes of interest

The term "seedlings" denotes possible propagation from other gardens by taking a small plant with the entire root system, or seedlings available in containers from a nursery.

For "division," gently loosen the soil around the entire plant with a trowel or shovel, lift the plant out of the ground gently, and then separate the plant into two by gently coaxing the roots apart.

"Cutting" means to cut a part of a stem or branch, usually before it becomes woody, and either soaking it in water until roots develop, or planting directly into the ground. For each plant that recommends cutting check with your nursery, native plant group, etc. to determine what should be done before you try it!

"Seeds" means the seeds of the plant are available for collection in quantities of ten per cent of that year's total production from other gardeners, the wild, or from nurseries.

THE CALIFORNIA FLORISTIC PROVINCE

The California Floristic Province is bounded by the crest of the Cascades and Sierra Nevada in the east; the Pacific Ocean, excluding the redwood forests in the west; the border with Baja in the south; and the Oregon border in the north.

There are many diverse elevations, climates, and habitats in the region.

CLIMATE

The California Floristic Province has three basic climatic zones: areas with cool summers, areas with hot summers, and areas with extremely hot summers, pretty much moving in three north/south strips from the coast, to intermediate valleys, to the eastern valleys of the region.

The winters vary in temperature from extreme winter cold, to mild sub-tropical conditions with little frost.

The Santa Anas have a huge impact on the native plants in the southern part of the Floristic Province. Just as they are preparing for their only moisture of the year, brought on by the rainy season, the Santa Ana winds will blow in hot, dry air, often bringing severe drought.

The Futterman's lush rock garden in the California Floristic Province at South Pasadena, California, is planted in a hollow to catch rain-water. The large rocks also help retain moisture. Planted exclusively with California natives, the garden has colour all year. This shot, taken in March, features the blooms of the knee-high Douglas iris (*Iris douglasiana*). *Andy Wasowski photo*

PLANT HISTORY

Native species follow this strip pattern, with more Mediterranean plants flourishing in the foggy summers of the coast, a mix of desert natives and coastal plants in the intermediate valleys, and only the desert-loving heat seekers in the east.

Before contact, the native plant species of the California Floristic Province thrived on shallow, rocky soil and arid summers. The local wildlife grazed on bunchgrasses. Since contact, and the onset of the excessive irrigation habits of Spanish and European settlers, watering the plants they brought from "home," most of the California natives have been, well, *drowned!*

The population boom in the west has meant the building of huge dams and canals, diversion of water from distant sources into the region, and the growth of commercial agriculture. All of which has taken its toll on native species.

Because water is now so scarce, many people have recognized the need for conservation, and have returned to drier, more native gardens.

The beautiful golden yarrow, also known as "Oregon Sunshine" (*Eriophyllum lanatum*), is native to the more open, dry areas of the Pacific Northwest, and the California Floristic Province. The plant's leaves have fine white hairs that reflect heat and reduce air movement across the leaves' surfaces, conserving water.
Kai Goodwin photo

PLANT QUIRKS

The native plants of the California Floristic Province have adapted to the severe conditions of its climate changes. Many annuals bloom and die back completely within the rainy season, to make sure they get enough water in their short life cycle. Some perennials shed their leaves in the dry season, reducing their need for water. Others have small, tough, waxy or hairy leaves that make it more difficult for the sun to extract moisture out of the plant.

Many dry summer plants spread their roots in a shallow fan, searching for any moisture in the top inches of the ground. Soil does not have to be deep or rich to grow California natives. The natural soil cover is acidic, shallow and poor in humus.

SITE PREPARATION

Before you plant your natives, remove existing plants from the patch you have chosen to transform first. Make sure that when you dig, all of the roots are raked and removed as well. In the coastal areas, you can also smother low-growing plants that are destined for removal by covering them with a thick mulch of leaves 15 centimetres (6 inches) deep, wood chips 8 centimetres (3 inches) deep, or newspaper (10 thicknesses deep). Then add topsoil to the depth of the root growth of your deepest-growing native plant. A less expensive and possibly more hassle-free way to go is to smother your existing plants with black plastic for a year before planting.

In the first year, deep and infrequent (every 7–10 days) watering will be needed to allow the plant's roots to establish themselves. Surround the new plants with some bark mulch, in dry times, to cut down on evaporation. You can put away the organic or chemical fertilizers and the lime. California natives like poor, dry, acidic soil.

After year one, shut off the taps completely. Natural fertilizer and mulches of fallen leaves and bark chips are all your plants should need; if not, you need to put in plants that like even less water!

CLASSIC, AVAILABLE, "EASY-TO-GROWS"

LOW: Under 60 cm (24 in)

Nodding Wild Onion (*Allium cernuum*)
Zone 4. 20–30 cm (8–12 in)
Purple, pink flowers
Perennial
Full sun, low water
Dry well-drained soil; from bulbs or seed
Native in different varieties to many parts of North America. Bulbs are edible
The city of Chicago was named from the Algonquin word for this plant: *chigagou*

California Fuchsia (*Zauschneria californica*)
a.k.a. hummingbird fuschia, hummingbird's trumpet, California firechalice
Zones 6–10. 15–20 cm (6–8 in)
Shrubby, pale green-grey-white leaves, trumpet-shaped scarlet flowers, capsule seed pods
Perennial
Full sun, low water
Sandy or rocky soil; root division or seed
Attracts hummingbirds
Cut it back to the ground in fall

Douglas Iris (*Iris douglasiana*)
Zones 8–10. 20–45 cm (8–18 in)
Glossy deep-green sword-shaped leaves
Lavender to deep blue orchidlike blossoms, elongated green skinned fruits
Perennial
Likes full sun, low water requirements

Well-drained soil; by root division
and rhizomes
Attracts bees, bumblebees, butterflies,
hummingbirds
Spreads in clumps, Greek for "rainbow"

Brodiaea (*Brodiaea* spp.)
Zones 7–10. 5–60 cm (2 in–2 ft)
Blue, purple, white, yellow, and pink flowers,
2–4 sword-shaped leaves
Perennial
Likes full sun/light shade, low water
Well-drained sandy soil; from seed or cormlets
Attracts butterflies and bees
Gophers like the bulblike corms; protect the
plants by placing the corms in wire baskets
before you plant

California Poppy (*Eschscholzia californica*)
Zones 8–10. 15–60 cm (6–24 in)
Vivid orange flowers, long hairy stalks, tan
hard-shelled seed pods
Perennial
Full sun, low water
Poor or dry sandy soil; from seeds, seedlings
Attracts bees
State flower

MEDIUM: 60–180 cm (2–6 ft)

Scarlet Monkeyflower (*Mimulus cardinalis*)
Zones 6–10. 60–120 cm (2–4 ft)
Swaying branches bear pale green leaves and
brilliant scarlet-red blossoms
Short-lived perennial
Light shade, high water
Sandy soil; by root division, seed, seedlings
Best planted in clumps
Attracts Anna's, Costa's, Allen's and rufous
hummingbirds, butterflies

Wild Buckwheat (*Eriogonum* spp.)
Zones 2–10. 8–120 cm (3 in–4 ft)
Shrubby, long lasting, woolly evergreen
leaves, white, pink, cream and yellow flowers
that fade to red
Evergreen
Full sun, low water
Dry sandy, loamy, rocky soil; from seedling,
seed, cuttings
Attracts seed-eating birds, butterflies, bees

Thistle sage (*Salvia carduacea*)
Zones 9–11. 10–90 cm (4 in–3 ft)
Whitish woolly leafless stem stacked with
clusters of vivid lavender flowers, pale green
fragrant leaves in a rosette at the base of the
stem, vermilion pollen sacs
Evergreen
Full sun, low water
Sandy or gravelly soil, from seeds, seedlings
Attracts hummingbirds, bees, birds

Lupine (*Lupinus* spp.)
Zones 3–10 for perennials; 5–10 for shrubby
species; all zones for annuals. 10–150 cm
(4 in–5 ft)
Blue, purple, cream, white flowers rise
above silvery palmlike leaves
Full sun, low–moderate water
Sandy soil; from soaked or stratified seed
Attracts bumblebees, butterflies
Many species; grows from tropics to tundra

Leopard Lily (*Lilium pardalinum*)
Zones 5–10. 90–180 cm (3–6 ft)
Slender stems, smooth-edged leaves, orange,
or red-orange flowers with purple spots, papery
seedpods
Perennial
Light shade, moderate water
Well-drained soil; from bulbs, divisions or seed

Attracts hummingbirds, butterflies, bumblebees
Gophers like these bulbs, too! Protect with
wire cages

Foothill Penstemon (*Penstemon heterphyllus*)
Zones 6–10. 30–75 cm (1–2.5 ft)
Long leafy stems; blue to purple flowers
Perennial, evergreen, short-lived (three years)
Full sun, low water
Well-drained sandy or rocky soil; from seed
Attracts native bees, wasps, hummingbirds
Mulch in cold zones, deadhead to prolong
blooms

TALL: 180 cm (6 ft) and over

Toyon (*Heteromeles arbutifolia*)
a.k.a. California holly, Christmas berry
Zone 8. 7.5–9 m (25–30 ft)
Glossy large leathery green leaves with cut-out
edges; small, fragrant, white flowers; tiny red
berries in winter
Evergreen shrub or small tree
Sun or partial shade, low water
Poor, dry soil and heat; from seedlings
Attracts birds, butterflies, bees
Subject to fire blight. Keep tools sanitized
(10% bleach, denatured alcohol) when pruning
out infected wood

Wild Lilac (*Ceanothus* spp.)
Zones 7–10. 60 cm–6 m (2–20 ft)
Dense fragrant clusters of blue, purple,
pink, or white flowers
Evergreen
Full sun, low water
Well-drained, rocky soil; from cuttings or
stratified seed
Attracts bees and butterflies, nesting birds, deer
Small ground covers to small multi-trunked trees

California Buckeye (*Aesculus californica*)
Zones 7–10. 3–9 m (10–30 ft)
Stalks of white, pale pink flowers rising
out of apple-green leaves
Deciduous
Full sun, low water
Well-drained soil; from seed
Attracts butterflies, hummingbirds, birds
Seeds poisonous to humans and bees

Blue Elderberry (*Sambucus mexicana*)
Zones 2–10. 3–13.5 m (10–45 ft)
Large shrub or small tree, large leaves,
fragrant clusters of yellow-white flowers
Deciduous
Full sun to light shade, moderate water
Well-drained soil; from rooted suckers,
cuttings, stratified seed
Attracts butterflies, bees, birds
Likes a high water table; plant in low
spot if well-drained

THE PACIFIC NORTHWEST

This Floristic Province continues north from the California Floristic Province, taking in the Redwood Forest and continuing in a band approximately 96 kilometres (60 miles) wide up the Pacific Coast through Oregon, Washington State, British Columbia, and Alaska to the crest of the Coastal, Cascade, and Sierra Nevada Mountain Ranges.

CLIMATE

The climate of the Pacific Northwest is definitely maritime. The winters are mild and rainy, the summers moderate in heat and fairly dry. The growing season is long as frost comes late in the fall. The Pacific Northwest can receive 150–325 centimetres (60–130 inches) of rain per year.

PLANT HISTORY

Before contact, Sitka spruce, western hemlock and redwoods ruled in this Floristic Province. The indigenous population did not have rotating "farms" as did their cousins inland; foraging provided enough fish, game and native plants to feed small villages.

Ferns, mosses, shooting stars, salal, bleeding hearts, etc. grew in shady areas. In clearings that enjoyed sun for parts of the day, Douglas iris, Oregon-grape, pink-flowering currant, ocean spray, Kinnikinnick, hairy manzanita, tiger lilies and nodding onion flourished. In particularly wet areas, one could find Labrador tea, bog rosemary, pacific rhododendron, western azalea, huckleberry, and Saskatoon serviceberry bushes. In fully exposed rocky or sandy areas, sedums, Nootka rose, and wild strawberries dominated.

Contact meant large-scale clearing of forests and a disruption of native flora and fauna. First contact was mostly by Europeans who brought their favourite plants from home.

The Pacific Northwest Floristic Province's climate ensures lush greenery, and this stream-side garden at the van Veenendaals' in Ladner, British Columbia, showcases a great variety of native and non-native plants. Natives include scarlet monkeyflower (*Mimulus cardinalis*) and Douglas iris (*Iris douglasiana*). *Edward van Veenendaal photo*

Some forests still stand, and many have been replanted as tree farms. Due to extreme water shortages in this temperate rain forest (Victoria, the capital city of British Columbia, had *all* watering of lawns and ornamental gardens banned in the summer of 2001), residents are beginning to turn to native plants for landscaping.

PLANT QUIRKS

This is a temperate rain forest. It's wet. Get used to it. Exotic English roses and such don't do well here. They mould, they blight, they drown! The natives of the Pacific Northwest, however, LOVE water, acidic soil and shade, unless they are beach or rock plants.

So make sure the shade lovers get enough of it, or they will do poorly. If you get over four hours of sun daily, plant the few natives that enjoy those bright conditions. If you need to make shade, plant quick-growing small trees and shrubs, and after a few years you will have created the climate for shade lovers.

The beautiful pink-flowered sea blush (*Plectritus congesta*), is accompanied here by the low-growing marsh violet (*Viola palustris*) in a Pacific Northwest yard. Together they make an excellent and colourful ground cover for low traffic areas. *Kai Goodwin photo*

SITE PREPARATION

"Same old" for removal of non-natives: dig them out, roots and all, or smother them with mulches of leaves: 30 cm (12 in); bark: 8 cm (3 in), or newspaper: (10 thicknesses). Please, don't be tempted by a Rototiller. You will be turning under millions of seeds of the non-natives and weed species that were on your property, and they will compete with your new plants for years!

Pacific Northwest native plants thrive on the acidic, poor, well-drained soil of the region. So the many amendments that you are used to adding to "beef up" your soil—fertilizers, lime—will no longer be necessary. In fact, too-rich soil can give natives "indigestion." To continue nature's grand design, don't rake up those leaves in the fall. Use them as a natural source of acid, fertilizer and mulch where they drop.

If you are lucky enough to have a furry green carpet of northwest moss on your property, learn to love it! People pay big bucks to have mosses put in their yards. It's the perfect ground cover: soft, green, zero maintenance and fairly traffic tolerant.

CLASSIC, AVAILABLE, "EASY-TO-GROWS"

LOW: Under 60 cm (24 in)

Kinnikinnick (*Arctostaphylos uva-ursi*)
a.k.a. bearberry in the east
Zone 4. 5–10 cm (2–4 in)
Glossy green leaves turn red in winter; white pink-tipped flowers, red fruits that look like small apples
Evergreen shrub
Sun or partial shade, low water
Dry, poor soil; from tip cuttings, seedlings
Attracts birds, butterflies, bees, bears, deer, coyotes
Each plant will spread 1.5 m (5 ft) or more

Northwestern Shooting Star
(*Dodecatheon dentatum*)
Zones 6–8. 15–40 cm (6–16 in)
White symmetrical dart-shaped flowers with
reddish-purple stamens forming point of dart
Perennial
Partial to full shade, moderate water
Moist soil; propagation from seeds

Lance-leaved Stonecrop
(*Sedum lanceolatum*)
Zone 5. 7.5–17.5 cm (3–7 in)
Clusters of small yellow flowers
Perennial, succulent
Full sun, little water
Dry, sandy or rocky soil; by seeds,
seedlings, or division
Sedum will spread on its own, making a
dense ground cover

Western Bleeding Heart (*Dicentra formosa*)
Zones 4–8. 45 cm (18 in)
Long blue-green leaves; nodding pink, white,
purple, rose heart-shaped flowers
Perennial
Partial sun or partial shade, moderate water
Moist, fertile soil; from seedlings and bare root
Attracts bees, butterflies

Nodding Wild Onion (*Allium cernuum*)
Zone 4. 20–30 cm (8–12 in)
Purplish-pink flowers
Perennial
Full sun, low water
Well-drained dry soil; by bulb
Attracts butterflies
Edible bulbs

Wild Strawberry (*Fragaria virginiana*)
Zone 5. 10–40 cm (4–16 ft)
Small white flowers and pale red berries
Perennial
Full sun, moderate water
Well-drained sandy soil; from seeds, seedlings, and bare root
Attracts bees, Canada geese, humans
Edible fruit

MEDIUM: 60–180 cm (2–6 ft)

Crimson Columbine (*Aquilegia formosa*)
Zones 7–10. 60–120 cm (2–4 ft)
Red and yellow flowers at ends of branches, several stems and divided leaves
Perennial
Partial to full sun, moderate water
Well-drained moist soil; from seed, seedlings
Attracts hummingbirds
"Formosa" means "beautiful" in Latin

Camas (*Camassia quamash*)
a.k.a. camas lily
Zones 7–10. 30–50 cm (12–20 in)
Narrow grasslike leaves, slender stem; light to deep blue-violet star-shaped flowers
Partial sun to partial shade, moderate water
Moist, well-drained soil; from bulbs
Attracts butterflies, bees
First peoples roasted or boiled the bulbs

Northern Maidenhair Fern
(*Adiantum pedatum*)
Zones 7–10. 30–60 cm (1–2 ft)
Fronds rise on stalk in fan formation
Perennial
Shade, moderate–high water
Poor, rocky soil; by division, seedlings

California Rosebay
(*Rhododendron macrophyllum*)
Zones 6–10. 150 cm–6 m (5–20 ft)
Evergreen shrub
Large green leaves, large pale purple flowers
Partial shade–partial sun, moderate water
Acidic, loamy soil; from seeds or seedlings
Attracts butterflies, hummingbirds

Salal (*Gaultheria shallon*)
Zones 7–10. 30 cm–3 m (1–10 ft)
Evergreen shrub, large leaves
Hanging bell-shaped pink and white flowers,
black, edible berries
Moderate sun–full shade, moderate–high water
Well-drained acidic loams and sand; by root
division, stratified seed
Attracts birds, hummingbirds, bears, bees

Nootka Rose (*Rosa nutkana*)
Zones 6–9. 180 cm (6 ft)
Perennial
Shrub, pink flowers, large purple hips
Partial–full sun, low water
Dry to moist soil; by offsets, seedlings
Attracts butterflies, hummingbirds, bees
The "hips" are packed with Vitamin C,
good in tea with honey

TALL: 180 cm (6 ft) and over

Evergreen Huckleberry (*Vaccinium ovatum*)
Zones 7–10. 120 cm–3 m (4–10 ft)
Evergreen shrub, small glossy leaves, pale
pink–white bell flowers, lush edible
blue–purple berries
Light–medium shade, moderate water
Well-drained acidic soil; from hardwood
cuttings or stratified seed
First peoples considered the berries candy
Great for pies

Pacific Flowering Dogwood (*Cornus nuttallii*)
a.k.a. Western Flowering Dogwood
Zones 6–10. To 6 m (20 ft)
Multi-stemmed trees, green oval leaves
at tips of branches turn reddish in fall,
soft white petals on flowers radiate from
pincushion centre
Deciduous
Partial shade, low water
Most soils; from seed, seedlings under
60 cm (2 ft)

Pink-flowering Currant (*Ribes sanguineum*)
Zones 7–10. 1.8–3 m (6–10 ft)
Small green leaves; hanging deep rose, pale pink
or white blossoms, purple berries in summer
Deciduous, light shade, low–moderate water
Well-drained soil; by cuttings in winter and
spring
Attracts hummingbirds, bees, butterflies
One of the first bloomers (March); a harbinger
of spring

Holly-leaf Cherry (*Prunus ilicifolia*)
Zones 7–10. 15 m (50 ft)
Dense shrub or multi-trunked tree;
bright green hollylike leaves, white blossoms,
large purple-red cherries
Evergreen
Full sun, low water
Well-drained rocky or sandy soil; from stratified
seed, hardwood cuttings
Attracts bees, butterflies, birds, squirrels

THE WESTERN MOUNTAINS AND BASINS

The Western Mountains and Basins Floristic Province begins at the crest of the Coastal, Cascade, and Sierra Nevada Ranges in the west, encompasses the Rocky Mountains, and continues east to the approximate midpoints (north-south) of Alberta, Montana, Wyoming, Colorado and New Mexico. This line, running up and down the middle of these states, forms the region's eastern border.

The area is characterized by its arid high mountains, and the dry valleys and broad basins that lie between them.

CLIMATE

The climate, like the elevation, varies greatly. The Great Basin of Nevada is often called a "cold desert," because it has little rainfall, 15–20 centimetres (6–8 inches) and cold temperatures, often reaching lows of -30° Celsius (-20° Fahrenheit) in winter.

Lower elevations get hot summers, higher elevations, cooler summer weather and temperature swings of up to thirty degrees in a single day! The region is considered arid because most of the water in the clouds coming in from the Pacific has dropped on the western slopes of the Sierra Nevada, Coastal and Cascade Ranges, leaving only 15–50 centimetres (6–20 inches) of annual rainfall for the Mountains and Great Basins region.

Soils are shallower as the elevation increases, and temperatures cool 5° F for every 300 metres (1000 feet) you climb.

PLANT HISTORY

The mountain slopes have drought- and cold-tolerant species such as ponderosa pine, limber pine, lodgepole pine, and Douglas-fir. Some deciduous species also grow on the slopes, such as quaking

aspen. The areas at the bases of the mountains are dominated by sagebrush, shrubs and herbs, and the lowlands by grasses and wildflowers. Moist areas grow Rocky Mountain columbine and mahonia, Saskatoon serviceberry, and fireweed. Dry, sunny areas support penstemons, wild white yarrow, blanket flower, and Indian pink.

PLANT QUIRKS

Mountain plants that are forced to grow on exposed sites with shallow, rocky soil, do so very slowly. They are low-growing perennials, with widespread root systems, or deep tap roots. Valley floors offer deeper, more nutritious soil and warmth in sheltered sunlight. These areas are dry, and the plants often succulents, or hairy, to reduce water loss. There are many differences in sunlight, moisture, elevation, and temperature in this climate. Plants that are adapted to the rich valley floors will not do well in exposed, rocky, windy sites. Attention is needed!

Lloyd Davies has planted a gorgeous rock garden that shouts with colour on his Western Mountains and Basins Floristic Province yard in Vernon, British Columbia, Canada. Here, various lewisias, also known as bitter-root, grace the rocks with their succulent water-storing leaves and their bright pink flowers.
Janet Armstrong photo

91

This shot shows what you can do in a dry creek bed: make it a beautiful garden by planting drought-lovers! Lloyd Davies has planted the area with various native and non-native species, including California poppy (*Eschscholzia californica*), bright pink phlox (*Phlox douglasii*) and pine-leaf penstemon (*Penstemon pinifolius*). Janet Armstrong photo

SITE PREPARATION

If exotic species are on your site, remove by digging out plant and roots, or smother with black plastic for one growing season before planting.

CLASSIC, AVAILABLE, "EASY-TO-GROWS"

LOW: Under 60 cm (24 in)

Wild White Yarrow
(*Achillea millefolium* var. *lanulosa*)
a.k.a. bloodwort, milfoil, nosebleed, woundwort
Zones 3–9.
White tiny fragrant flowers in flat cluster at top of green stalk

Perennial, 30–60 cm (1–2 ft)
Full sun–part shade, moderate water
Most soils, from seed or division
Attracts butterflies
First peoples use this plant for a variety of
medicinal purposes from coughs to fever

Western Blue Flag (*Iris missouriensis*)
Zones 2–6. 60 cm (2 ft)
Tall green swordlike leaves, blue flag flowers
Perennial
Full sun, high water in spring, low in
summer and fall
Wide range of soil; by root division after
blooming
Attracts bees, hummingbirds
Hummingbirds steal nectar from the iris
without pollinating it: "nectar thieves"

Wild Four O'clock (*Mirabilis multiflora*)
a.k.a. Colorado four o'clock
Zones 5–20. To 90 cm (3 ft)
Shrublike; many magenta flowers
Perennial
Full sun–light shade, low water
Well-drained sandy soil; from seed, small root
pieces in fall
Attracts pollinating insects
Flowers open in the midafternoon, thus their
name

Mosquito Plant (*Agastache cana*)
Zones 5–8. 90 cm (3 ft)
Bushy clump of leafy stalks supporting
fragrant bright pink spiked flowers
Perennial
Full sun, moderate water
Most soil; from seed, cuttings
Attracts moths, hummingbirds
Smells like bubblegum

Indian Pink (*Silene laciniata*)
a.k.a. Mexican campion
Zones 4–8. 30–60 cm (1–2 ft)
Red, flaring, jagged-edged flowers
Perennial
Full sun–light shade, moderate water
Most well-drained soil; from stratified seed
A hummingbird's favourite

Creeping Mahonia (*Mahonia repens*)
a.k.a. creeping holly grape
Zones 4–9. 30–90 cm (1–3 ft)
Low growing; hollylike leaves, fragrant yellow
flowers; berries in summer/fall
Evergreen
Full sun–full shade, low–high water
All soils, high traffic; from seed or pieces of
established plants
Attracts fruit-eating birds, small mammals
First peoples used roots, leaves for medicinal
purposes, to treat rheumatism, liver disorders,
stomach aches

Showy Goldeneye (*Viguiera multiflora*)
Zones 3–6. 30–90 cm (1–3 ft)
Numerous golden-yellow flowers with
bright gold centres
Perennial
Full sun–part shade, moderate water
Most soils; from seed
Attracts butterflies, bees

Rocky Mountain Columbine
(*Aquilegia caerulea*)
Zones 3–8. 30–60 cm (1–2 ft)
Bushy plants with long spurs of blue and white
flowers
Perennial
Shade to partial sun, moderate water
Most soils; from seeds, seedlings
Attracts hummingbirds, butterflies
Colorado State flower

MEDIUM: 60–180 cm (2–6 ft)

Indian Blanket Flower (*Gaillardia aristata*)
Zones 3–9. 60–90 cm (2–3 ft)
Bright yellow and red flowers growing above
mounds of coarse, hairy foliage
Perennial
Full sun, low–moderate water
Wide range of soils; from seed
Attracts bees and butterflies
Member of the daisy family, deadhead to
prolong blooms

Sideoats Grama (*Bouteloua curtipendula*)
Zones 3–10. 30–90 cm (1–3 ft)
Blue green while growing, golden to light
brown in fall; seeds droop on the sides of
zigzag stems
Perennial
Full sun, low–moderate moisture
Dry soils; from seed
Attracts coyotes, foxes, butterflies,
meadowlarks
Seed heads attractive in dried flower
arrangements

Datil (*Yucca baccata*)
a.k.a. banana yucca
Zones 5–10. To 90 cm (3 ft)
Machete-like leaves, banana-shaped fruit;
forms a low thicket
Evergreen
Full sun, low water
Well-drained dry soil; from seed or offsets
taken from plants
Attracts moths, birds, and small mammals
First peoples used twined leaves to make cord
for shoes, mats, nets, roots to make soap, the
fruits for food raw or roasted

Fireweed (*Epilobium angustifolium*)
a.k.a. willow-herb
Zones 2–9. 120–150 cm (4–5 ft)
Tall stalks with narrow leaves and pink
bright flowers in spikes
Perennial
Full sun–full shade, high water
Well-drained moist soils; from seed,
root shoots in spring
Attracts bumblebees
A beekeeper's favourite

Golden-beard Penstemon
(*Penstemon barbatus*)
a.k.a. beardlip penstemon
Zones 2–9. 90–120 cm (3–4 ft)
Tall sparsely leafed stems support scarlet
tubular flowers
Perennial
Full sun, low–moderate water
Dry, well-drained soil; from seeds
Attracts hummingbirds
Have yellow hairs at flower's opening—
the "beard"

Rabbitbrush (*Chrysothamnus* spp.)
Zones 2–10. 60–180 cm (2–6 ft)
Greenish-grey shrub with brilliant
yellow flowers
Deciduous
Full sun, low water
Dry, well-drained soils; from seed
Attracts bees, butterflies, house finches,
pine siskins
Prune in fall for more compact plant with
more flowers

Golden Currant (*Ribes aureum*)
a.k.a. buffalo currant
Zones 2–9. 60–180 cm (2–6 ft)
A shrub with fragrant golden-yellow flowers

Deciduous
Full sun–part shade, moderate water
Most soils; from seed
Attracts squirrels, chipmunks, bears, racoons, birds, butterflies.
First peoples used the berries dried, fresh or made into jelly

Apache Plume (*Fallugia paradoxa*)
Zones 5–10. 120–180 cm (4–6 ft)
Dark green leaves, silver undersides; clusters of white blossoms, feathery pink seed-heads
Semi-evergreen shrub
Full–partial sun; low water
Poor soil; from seeds, seedlings

TALL: 180 cm (6 ft) and over

Saskatoon Serviceberry (*Amelanchier alnifolia*)
a.k.a. Juneberry, shadblow, shadbush, serviceberry
Zones 2–7. 90 cm–12 m (3–40 ft)
Thicket-forming bush, white flowers, delicious berries
Deciduous
Full sun–part shade, moderate water
Most soils; from seed or rooted from suckers
Attracts deer, squirrels, chipmunks, birds, butterflies
Berries are good for jelly

Big Sagebrush (*Artemisia tridentata*)
Zones 4–10. 30 cm–4.5 m (1–15 ft)
Fragrant silver-coloured leaves, tiny clusters of flowers
Evergreen
Full sun–part shade, low water
Well-drained dry soil; from seed
Attracts aphids, ladybugs, rabbits and small mammals
An allergen

Quaking Aspen (*Populus tremuloides*)
Zones 1–7. 12–18 m (40–60 ft)
Medium-sized trees in groves, white bark,
leaves flutter in the wind, turn brilliant
yellow in fall
Deciduous, full sun, high water requirements
Wide range of soils; transplant seedlings as
long as water available
Attracts large variety of birds and animals,
from owls to elk to woodpeckers to bluebirds

Riverbank Grape (*Vitis riparia*)
Zones 3–8. To 6 m (20 ft) plus
Rambling vine bearing large clusters
of blue grapes
Deciduous
Full sun, high water requirements
Range of soils; near fresh water; by seed,
seedling
Attracts squirrels, raccoons, 100 species of birds
First peoples cultivated riverbank grape for
the fruit

Pinyon Pine (*Pinus edulis*)
Zones 4–8. 3–12 m (10–40 ft)
Large shrubs or small trees,
bushy needles, seeds
Evergreen
Full sun, moderate–low water
Well-drained soil; from seedling
Attracts jays, especially the pinyon jay,
other birds, squirrels, bears and humans!
Edible seeds

THE SOUTHWESTERN DESERTS

The Southwestern Deserts of North America follow the border between the USA and Mexico, starting in southeastern California, and encompassing southern Nevada, southern Arizona, southern New Mexico, and southwest Texas.

Elevation ranges from 1500 m (5000 ft) above sea level in the Chihuahuan Desert, to near sea level in the Sonoran desert.

CLIMATE

This region has three main deserts: The Mohave, the Sonoran and the Chihuahuan. The Mohave is the smallest, and it has lows in winter of -17° to -12° C (0–10° F), and very hot summers. Rain and snowfall account for the 5–25 centimetres (2–10 inches) of annual precipitation. Its elevations range from sea level to 1200 metres (4000 feet).

The Sonoran Desert is the warmest in the region, with winter lows of -17° to 1° C (0–30° F). Its highest point is around 900 metres (3000 feet), and its lowest is at sea level. Rainfall here is 5–30 centimetres (2–12 inches).

The Chihuahuan Desert is as cold in its northern range as the Great Basin, reaching winter lows of -26° C (-15° F). It is considered the "high" desert. Its lowest elevation is 750 metres (2500 feet), and its highest is 1500 metres (5000 feet). The Chihuahuan actually has heavy summer rains, and an annual precipitation of 12.5–35 centimetres (5–14 inches).

In all but the Chihuahuan, there is little precipitation, and when it does fall, high winds and full sun evaporate the drops quickly. So water is scarce. And in urban areas, cement and pavement hold the heat. Where temperatures used to drop at night, the man-made materials now bring about twenty-four-hour-a-day warmth.

Wynn and Kym Anderson of El Paso, Texas, live in the foothills of the Chihuahuan Desert. They transformed a conventional lawn and exotic plant landscape into one that is almost entirely native. Of the exotics, only the Russian Mulberry remains. Most of the natives were grown from seed that Wynn collected from the surrounding desert, including the yellow sierra sundrops (*Calylophus hartwegii*), foreground, the silver-leaved shrub Texas butterflybush (*Buddleia marrubiifolia*), background, and the small red-flowered shrub autumn sage (*Salvia greggii*). *Andy Wasowski photo*

Soil is alkaline, often hardpan and salty, and very poor in organic material. No wonder lawns have such a hard time here, and people are fighting over water use!

As with all other Floristic Provinces, it is important to choose plant communities whose individuals are companionable with each other and with your particular site. Desert plants are choosy and often will not survive transplantation, even from nursery-purchased seedlings.

PLANT HISTORY

In the Mohave, the Joshua tree, torry mesquite, and cholla are signature plants. The Sonoran is known for its palo verde, desert willow, sages, and the beautiful saguaro. The Chihuahuan Desert is known for its smaller cacti, littleleaf sumac, honey mesquite, and blackfoot daisy.

Before contact, there were no ornamental gardens. First peoples grew corn and beans, taught by their southern cousins, foraged for native plants for food, medicinal and ceremonial purposes, and hunted wildlife.

Early Europeans who were not accustomed to the constant exposure, closed in courtyards to shield themselves from the sun and dusty wind, and by mid-twentieth century pumped in water to make the desert more like "home." Water and labour were cheap, and full formal bluegrass lawns, large shade trees, and exotic flower gardens were *de rigueur* for anybody who was anybody.

This environmentally disastrous practice has only begun to fade out in the past decade, as water and labour have become hot commodities. Today, native plants are becoming much more popular.

PLANT QUIRKS

Plants of this region define "adapt or die." They have evolved to withstand drought and heat in amazing ways. Some plants have silver leaves that reflect light and heat. Some have waxy leaves that hold whatever moisture comes their way, while still others have tiny leaves, minimizing evaporation.

Some plants are "drought deciduous," dropping their leaves when water is scarce, thus reducing the plant's need for moisture, while others remain leafless for most of the season, photosynthesizing with the chlorophyll in their stems. Then there are the succulents, with veritable water storehouses built into each leaf to keep the plants hydrated in severe drought.

The seed coats of some the natives in this region are tough, and contain their own growth regulators that will only allow germination when the conditions are right. Other plants go to seed in rhythm with the seasonal rains.

"Desert plants are choosy!" Unfortunately, for all their hardiness, when it comes to growing where we want to place them, this rings all too true. The saguaro cactus is the definitive southwestern cactus. *Everyone* wants one in their garden. But just try to propagate or transplant one from a nursery: 50% chance of survival, at best. Others will do well until their roots get a little too soggy during the first year of drip irrigation to settle them in. They will turn brown at their base—too much water—the most common killer of cacti.

Unlike other plants, cacti prefer to stay completely dry after transplantation; put away the water can.

SITE PREPARATION

Dig up that lawn, roots and all, and compost it! Or use the smother-with-black-plastic method if you don't mind waiting one year to plant.

Try not to garden in containers, if possible, and if you have room, take your desert plants out of containers and put them in the earth. They like it much better. If you must have container plants, make sure that the containers have a large, unobstructed, drainage hole in the bottom or the plant will get too wet, rot, and die.

If your plants don't like cold winter temperatures, cover them up.

Always plant in soil with excellent drainage, and when planting out a cactus, make sure that soil completely surrounds the roots. Don't leave any air pockets.

Once roots are established, water deeply once every 10 days for a couple of months, and if the temperatures are extreme while the plant is in this vulnerable stage—too hot, or too cold, cover them up for protection.

When planting agaves and yuccas, same water treatment; don't do it! They also prefer dry roots while acclimatizing. Some agaves and yuccas also appreciate a cover in weather that is too hot at this stage in their life cycles. Ask your nursery if the one you have chosen is in this category.

In general, water desert plants only when they have established roots and the weather is warm. And then water deeply and infrequently to help roots grow deep.

There is no need to shovel in gravel and place a few isolated cacti here and there in your yard, unless that's attractive to you. There are a variety of many beautiful native plants in this region. A native desert garden can have small trees, flowering and evergreen shrubs, succulents, grasses and flowers.

What is essential is to plant according to the conditions of your particular site.

Remember, "Desert plants are choosy!"

CLASSIC, AVAILABLE, "EASY-TO-GROWS"

LOW: Under 60 cm (24 in)

Claretcup Cactus
(*Echinocereus triglochidiatus*)
a.k.a. Mojave mound
Zone 9. 20–30 cm (8–12 in)
Cylindrical cactus, large white spines, large brilliant orange, red, magenta flowers, red fruits
Evergreen
Full sun, low water
Excellent drainage, dry soil; by seed, tissue culture, division, nursery seedling
Attracts hummingbirds, orioles, butterflies, song birds, doves, desert mammals. Many are harvested illegally. Ask to see a propagation permit

Desert Marigold (*Baileya multiradiata*)
Zones 8–10. 30–45 cm (12–18 in)
Blue-green leaves and stems, multi-layered yellow flowers, yellow centres
Evergreen
Full sun, low–moderate water
Good drainage; from seeds, will self-sow
Attracts butterflies, bees, birds, rabbits, lizards
Individuals short-lived, but communities continue through self-seeding

Golden Columbine (*Aquilegia chrysantha*)
Zones 8–10. 30–90 cm (1–3 ft)
Yellow, fragrant, tubular flowers
Full sun, low water
Good drainage, dry soils; from seed, seedlings
Attracts hummingbirds
Exquisite!

Desert Zinnia (*Zinnia grandiflora*)
Zones 5–10. 15–20 cm (6–8 in)
Ground cover of tough, wiry grasslike green leaves, bursts of yellow daisies that are dry straw colour

Perennial
Full sun, low water
Dry soil; by division, seedlings
Attracts butterflies
Very tough ground cover

Mexican Evening Primrose
(*Oenothera berlandiera*)
Zones 5–10. 30–45 cm (12–18 in)
Saucer-shaped pink flowers
Sun or shade, low water
Poor, dry soil; by division or seedlings
Excellent ground cover
Attracts butterflies; open in daylight

Blackfoot daisy
(*Melampodium leucanthum*)
a.k.a. rock daisy
Zones 5–10. 30–45 cm (12–18 in)
Mounds of grey-green leaves, small
white daisies, yellow centres
Perennial
Sun–partial shade, low water
Dry, poor soil; heat; by seedling or seeds
Attracts butterflies
Sensitive to overwatering

MEDIUM: 60–180 cm (2–6 ft)

Dorri sage (*Salvia dorrii*)
Zones 8–10. 60–90 cm (2–3 ft)
Fragrant pale bluish-grey leaves, flowers
of neon blue petals, yellow stamens, in balls
of reddish purple
Evergreen or cold deciduous
Full-day sun, moderate water
Well-drained sandy soil; cuttings or seed
Attracts hummingbirds, butterflies, bees
Aromatic leaves, can be used as an herb
for cooking

Pink Fairy Duster (*Calliandra eriophylla*)
a.k.a. mesquitillo
Zone 9. 60–120 cm (2–4 ft)
Multi-branched shrub with profuse pink
flowers, look like their name
Evergreen if kept moist, drought deciduous,
or cold deciduous
Full sun, moderate water
Well-drained soil; from root cuttings, seed,
or nursery seedlings
Attracts deer, birds, butterflies, bees
Blooms after rain; useful for controlling erosion

Teddy Bear Cholla (*Opuntia bigelovii*)
a.k.a. jumping cactus
Zones 7–10. 60–150 cm (2–5 ft)
Cylindrical joints covered in 2.5 cm (1 in) spines
and yellow, orange, pink or magenta flowers,
mauve or yellow fruits
Evergreen
Full sun, low water
Dry soil; by cuttings, seedlings, bare root
Attracts bees, desert mammals, birds
In drought, animals eat the pads as a source
of water

Bush Dalea (*Dalea pulchra*)
Zone 9. 90–150 cm (3–5 ft)
Evergreen, cold deciduous, or drought
deciduous
Purple flowers on short shrub
Full sun, moderate water
Limestone and rocky soil; by fresh seed or
semi-hardwood cuttings
Attracts butterflies, bumblebees, squirrels

Brittlebrush (*Encelia farinosa*)
a.k.a. incienso
Zones 9–10. 60–180 cm (2–6 ft)
Mounded bush of grey leaves, tall stalks,
hundreds of brilliant yellow daisies

Evergreen or drought deciduous
Full sun, low–moderate water
Dry well-drained soil; from seed, self-sows
Attracts chuckwallas, songbirds, deer mice
Dried branches are burned as incense

Chuparosa (*Justicia californica*)
Zones 9–10. 150–240 cm (5–8 ft)
Hundreds of small red flowers on
evergreen stems
Evergreen shrub
Full sun–dappled shade, moderate water
Well-drained soil; from softwood cuttings
Attracts hummingbirds, butterflies, orioles,
warblers, goldfinches
Great trailed up and over trellises

TALL: 180 cm (6 ft) and over

Joshua Tree (*Yucca brevifolia*)
Zone 8. 6–9 m (20–30 ft)
Tall tree yucca, stiff blue-green leaves, white
flowers every few years
Evergreen, full sun, low water
Good drainage, dry sandy soil; from fresh seed
pressed into sand
Seedlings need protection from mule deer,
rabbits, wood rats, and ground squirrels
Attracts songbirds, doves, lizards, woodpeckers,
butterflies and moths
Check nursery permits!

Blue Palo Verde (*Cercidium floridum*)
Zones 9–10. 4.5–9 m (15–30 ft)
Yellow flowers, lime-green leaves, pale blue-
green trunks, short bean-pod-like fruits
Drought and cold deciduous
Full sun, moderate water
Fast-draining swale, along washes in hot climates
From fresh seed, seedlings, ball & burlap
Attracts bees and butterflies
Beautiful, gnarled branches

Ocotillo (*Fouquieria splendens*)
Zones 8–10. 3.6–7.5 m (12–25 ft)
Bush of tall spiny multi-leaved individual
stems topped with large red–orange flowers
Perennial
Full sun, low water
Dry, well-drained soil; from seed or cutting
Attracts hummingbirds, orioles, butterflies, bees
Overwatering invites fungi

Desert Willow (*Chilopsis linearis*)
Zones 7–10. 4.5–12 m (15–40 ft)
Multi-trunked tree, willowlike leaves,
fragrant tubular pink, rose, purple flowers,
string-bean-sized fruit
Winter deciduous, drought deciduous
Full sun, high water
Moist soil (swale); by seed, seedlings
Attracts hummingbirds, doves, pigeons,
butterflies, bees
Not a true willow (begonia family), but a
beauty! Prune suckers in summer

Honey Mesquite
(*Prosopis glandulosa* var. *glandulosa*)
Zones 8–10. 6–10.5 m (20–35 ft)
Multi-trunked, slender leaves, cone-shaped
yellow fuzzy flowers, bright red bean pods
Winter deciduous
Full sun, moderate water
Good drainage; by seedling
Attracts bees, butterflies, birds
Forms thickets, good for barriers

THE GREAT PLAINS

The Great Plains, or Prairies, form the "heartland" of North America, ranging from northwestern Alberta, eastern Montana, eastern Wyoming, eastern Colorado and eastern Texas to central Ontario, Minnesota, Illinois, southeastern Missouri, Northwestern Aransas, and all but the southeast and southwest of Texas. All but the badlands of the Dakotas are flat rolling rises and valleys.

CLIMATE

Rainfall is moderate and wetlands are rare, occurring only along river banks, and in depressions called prairie potholes. Winds and exposure evaporate water, and produce high alkalinity and salinity.

PLANT HISTORY

The prairies were once a huge, uninterrupted grassland of more than 1.8 million square kilometres (700,000 square miles). The soil was so rich, farmers moved in and stayed, decimating the wildlife and grasses, and exhausting and eroding the soil. Today,

A sample of a Canadian prairie wildflower garden at the home of Shirley Froehlich, St. Andrews, Manitoba, shows black-eyed Susans (*Rudbeckia hirta*), western yarrow (*Achillea millefolium*), giant hyssop (*Agastache foeniculum*) and blue flag iris (*Iris versicolor*), among other natives.
Shirley Froehlich photo

Pat Armstrong planted this prairie on her corner lot in Chicago, Illinois, twenty years ago. In order for the garden to become successfully established, she weeded carefully for the first three years. Maintenance now consists of a burn each March. Species include the pale purple coneflower (*Echinacea pallida*) by the front door, and butterfly milkweed. In autumn, goldenrods and asters are set off by the gold and pink hues of big bluestem (*Andropogon gerardii*), and Indian grass (*Sorghastrum nutans*). Andy Wasowski photo

only a small fraction of untouched prairie remains.

There are three distinct regions within this Floristic Province:

- Shortgrass, western prairie;
- Mixed grass, central prairie; and
- Tall grass, eastern prairie.

The shortgrass prairie is dry, with only 25–50 centimetres (10–20 inches) of precipitation a year. The grasses native to this area are blue grama, buffalo grass, and needle-and-thread grass.

The mixed-grass prairies were once divided into north and south regions. The north region took in the Canadian prairies and Montana, the Dakotas, eastern Wyoming, and parts of Nebraska. The grasses native to that region are little bluestem, needle-and-thread, Junegrass and blue grama. The southern mixed-grass prairie passes through the centre of Kansas, Oklahoma, and Texas, and into northeastern Mexico. Moisture here is more dependable, and supports little bluestem, sideoats grama, and blue grama.

The tall grass prairies once covered 572,000 square kilometres (220,000 square miles). Less than 1% exists today. Native grasses include big bluestem, prairie dropseed, Indian grass, little bluestem, and sideoats grama.

Prairie fires were an essential part of the life cycle of the prairie. First peoples burned areas of grasses to lure buffalo and bison to the fresh, tender grass shoots that would spring up after a fire.

Fires, both natural and man-made, burned away old debris, and released nutrients, stimulating root systems for strong new plants. Today, fires are not absolutely essential to prairie gardeners, and can be dangerous. Some landscaping and prairie restoration companies provide this service; they know what they're doing, and will have the proper permits. Always check for proper permits, and have all necessary safety gear on hand.

Today's gardeners, because of the small size of their "prairie," can easily weed by hand-pulling woody plants and mowing the grasses once a year, in the spring.

PLANT QUIRKS

You will need at least half a day of sun on your site and lots of air circulation for a true prairie garden.

Seeding of prairie grasses requires firm contact with the soil. The method should be direct-seed, roller, and mulch. No need for soil amendments, unless your soil is completely devoid of organic matter.

Buffalo grass is an excellent lawn replacement. It has lived on the Great Plains for centuries, evolving efficient water use and sod-forming ability. And you can mow it to look like a "real" lawn! Mow buffalo grass with sharp blades at three-week intervals to a height of 2.5 inches.

SITE PREPARATION

Dig out completely or smother existing species with organic or plastic mulch before you plant.

THE GRASSES

Prairie grasses need good bed preparation: removal of all roots of former inhabitants and cultivated but rich firm clay or loam soils. If your soil is lacking in nutrients, consider planting a "green manure" of buckwheat for the winter before you plant your prairie grass. This will naturally add nitrogen to your soil. You can keep your soil well fed by adding compost as a mulch anytime.

Some prairie grasses are now available in seed, plugs (be sure to get pre-rooted) and sod. All are best planted in well-tilled soil in the early spring. To minimize transplant shock of plugs and sod, you can fertilize first with .5 kilogram (1 pound) each of phosphorous and nitrogen per 90 square metres (1000 square feet), and keep moist with drip irrigation until established. After that, TURN OFF THE WATER!

Grass seed needs excellent contact with the soil for full germination. You can use a roller after you seed to optimize the contact.

Make sure that plugs and sod have good, deep root formation before you buy.

Also make sure that you keep weeds out of the bed until the grasses thicken up.

An easy but costly way to start a new prairie grass bed over an existing lawn or garden is to cover it with leaves 12 inches deep, or 10 sheets of newspaper, topped by a few inches of weed-free topsoil, and start planting!

THE FLOWERS

Native prairie flower seeds are best planted in fall. Stay away from those "wildflowers-in-a-can" products. See Chapter Six: Specialty Gardens.

CLASSIC, AVAILABLE, "EASY-TO-GROWS"

LOW: Under 60 cm (24 in)

Blue Grama (*Bouteloua gracilis*)
Zones 5–8. 15–30 cm (6–12 in)
Bunchgrass, blue-green seed-heads shaped like eyebrows on stalks
Perennial grass
Full sun, low water
Dry, poor soils; from seeds, seedlings
Attracts birds, mice, and voles
Use seed-heads in dried flower arrangements

Little Bluestem (*Schizachyrium scoparium*)
Zones 3–8. 45–75 cm (1.5–2.5 ft)
Grass with fine blue-green blades in spring and summer, bronze-red in fall, fluffy seed-heads
Perennial grass
Full sun, low water
Poor, dry soil; seeds, bare root, seedlings
Attracts birds and butterflies
Use dried heads in flower arrangements

Buffalo Grass (*Buchloe dactyloides*)
Zones 5–10. 7.5–12.5 cm (3–5 in)
Sage green, fine, soft bladed, tan and stiff in winter
Sun or partial shade, low water
Poor, dry soil; from seeds, plugs
Attracts birds
Excellent grass for lawns, when mowed, ornamental when left

Dotted Gayfeather (*Liatris punctata*)
Zones 3–10. 15–60 cm (6–24 in)
Upright green feathery stems, pink feathery
flowers
Perennial
Full sun, low water
Well-drained dry soil; from seeds, bare root
seedlings
Attracts bees, butterflies
Cut flowers for bouquets

Rose Verbena (*Verbena canadensis*)
Zones 5–10. 15 cm (6 in)
Low-growing, green leaves, pink flowers
Perennial
Full sun, low–moderate water
Well-drained soil; from seed or seedlings
Attracts butterflies
Will self-sow in open ground

Missouri Evening Primrose
(*Oenothera missouriensis*)
Zones 4–8. 20–25 cm (8–10 in)
Low-growing with fragrant, canary
yellow flowers
Perennial
Full sun, low water
Dry soil; from seeds
Attracts birds and butterflies
Excellent choice on smaller dry yards

Aromatic Aster (*Aster oblongifolius*)
a.k.a. savoury-leaved aster
Zones 3–6. 40 cm (16 in)
Fine, green-blue foliage, flowers of sky-blue
rays, yellow centres
Perennial
Full sun, low water
Poor, dry soil; from seeds, seedlings
Attracts butterflies, bees
Excellent ground cover

MEDIUM: 60–180 cm (2–6 ft)

Indian Grass (*Sorghastrum nutans*)
Zones 3–9. 90–180 cm (3–6 ft)
Graceful stalks and seed heads, green in
summer, bronze in fall, bronze flowers
Perennial grass
Full sun, low water
Poor soil; heat; from seeds, seedlings,
bare root
Attracts birds
Mow or burn in spring to remove old growth

Big Bluestem (*Andropogon gerardii*)
a.k.a. turkey foot
Zones 3–8. 90–240 cm (3–8 ft)
Tall bunchgrass, red stem in summer,
crimson in fall, flowerheads three-pronged
Perennial grass
Full sun, all water
Poor soil; from seeds, seedlings
Attracts birds, deer, butterflies
Mow or burn in spring

Purple Coneflower (*Echinacea purpurea*)
a.k.a. prairie coneflower
Zones 3–7. 30–50 cm (12–20 in)
Drooping flower of pink rays of petals,
central cone of burgundy
Perennial
Full sun, low water
Poor, dry soil; from seeds or seedlings
Attracts butterflies, birds
Use flowers or seed-heads in flower
arrangements; used for herbal remedy
to boost immune system

Wild Bergamot (*Monarda fistulosa*)
a.k.a. wild monardo, Oswego tea, oregano, etc.
Zones 3–9. 60–90 cm (2–3 ft)
Upright stems holding clusters of
pinkish-purple tubular flowers
Perennial
Full sun–part shade, moderate water
Moist soil; from seed, plant division
Attracts butterflies, bees, moths
First peoples used this plant as an antibiotic

Blue Sage (*Salvia azurea*)
Zones 4–10. 90–120 cm (3–4 ft)
Tall green stalks, small leaves, light blue flowers
Perennial
Full sun, moderate water
Dry soil; from seed, root division, cuttings
Attracts bees, butterflies, hummingbirds
Use leaves as herbs in cooking

Cardinal Flower (*Lobelia cardinalis*)
a.k.a. scarlet lobelia
Zones 2–9. 60–270 cm (2–9 ft)
Spikes of up to 50 crimson-red flowers per stalk
Perennial
Sun–partial shade, high moisture
Wet sites, fertile soil; by division, seed
Attracts hummingbirds
Named for the Roman Catholic cardinal's
red robes

Soapweed (*Yucca glauca*)
Zones 4–8. 90 cm (3 ft)
Tough shrub with sword-like leaves,
tall stalks of showy whitish flowers
Evergreen
Full sun, low water
Most soils, from seed, offsets
Attracts butterflies and moths
Roots pounded for soap by first peoples

Wood's Rose (*Rosa woodsii*)
Zones 3–8. 90 cm (3 ft)
Low-growing shrub, deep-green leaves, pink
flowers, red fall fruit. Foliage turns burnt orange
in fall
Deciduous
Full sun–light shade, moderate water
Most soils; from seedlings, root division,
cuttings
Attracts deer, birds, bees
Fruit "hips" high in Vitamin C

TALL: 180 cm (6 ft) and over

Bur Oak (*Quercus macrocarpa*)
a.k.a. mossy cup oak
Zones 3–8. 21–24 m (70–80 ft)
Large singular trunk, large branches,
rounded leaves, acorns with large caps
Deciduous
Full sun, moderate water
Most soils; from stratified seed, seedlings,
ball & burlap
Attracts squirrels, wild turkeys, chipmunks
and many other seed-gatherers
Slow-growing: a plant for the future

Chokecherry (*Prunus virginiana*)
Zones 2–8. 3–7.5 m (10–25 ft)
Thicket-forming shrub, white cylindrical
clusters of flowers, sour red berries
Deciduous
Full sun, moderate water
Well-drained soil; from seed
Attracts racoons, birds, butterflies
First peoples used the bark to treat coughs,
fever, arthritis

Downy Hawthorn (*Crataegus mollis*)
Zones 3–8. 6–9 m (20–30 ft)
Multi-trunked tree, large spreading canopy, pink
or white blossoms, red fruits, red or yellow fall
colour
Deciduous
Full sun, moderate water
Most soils; from nursery seedlings, ball & burlap
Attracts birds, butterflies
A knockout and historical—Christ's crown
of thorns

Eastern Cottonwood (*Populus deltoides*)
Zones 3–9. 22–30 m (75–100 ft)
Tall tree with brilliant yellow fall leaves
Full sun, high water
Most soils; from seed, seedlings, twig cuttings,
ball & burlap
Attracts birds, butterflies
In the wild, found by streams

Trumpet Creeper (*Campsis radicans*)
Zones 5–9. 9–12 m (30–40 ft)
Large rambling vine, red-orange trumpet
flowers, expansive
Deciduous
Full sun, moderate water
Most soils; from stratified seeds,
softwood cuttings
Attracts hummingbirds, other birds
Great for a trellis, fence, or arbour

THE EASTERN WOODLANDS

The northern border of the Eastern Woodlands takes in the Canadian maritime provinces, southern Quebec and Ontario, goes as far west as the western shores of the Great Lakes and the centre lines of Minnesota, Wisconsin, Illinois, and touches the southeast and northeast tips of Arkansas in the west. This Floristic Province's southernmost border extends to Northern Virginia and Tennessee.

CLIMATE

The climate varies greatly across this large region. The average rainfall is high and summers are warm and humid. Winters are cold, and the mostly deciduous trees drop their leaves.

The heat and humidity of the summer months bring with them lush growth, but also fungus, bacteria, and the potential for rot. South-facing slopes warm up faster in spring, and retain heat longer in fall.

There are as many soil conditions as there are climatic changes and elevations, ranging from dry and shallow on ridgetops, to deep black moist soil

Virginia bluebells (*Mertensia virginica*) carpet the yard of the VanDeKerckhove's home in Springfield, Illinois. This native of the Eastern Woodlands Floristic Province provides a beautiful alternative ground cover to conventional turf grass.
Chris Young photo

in valley bottoms. Some soil is gravel or hardpan clay, too dense to work. In the forest, fallen leaves provide mulch and fertilizer.

Evergreens flourish at the northernmost border of the region, where temperatures drop and the growing seasons are shorter. To the south, the humid hot weather of the Coastal Plains nurtures more pines. To the west, as the rainfall drops, prairie grasses take over.

PLANT HISTORY

For thousands of years, Eastern Woodlands first peoples lived in the deciduous forests, hunting, fishing, foraging and clearing small areas of land for "casual" gardens, allowing the forest to move back in as they moved on each year.

The first immigrants cleared large parts of the forests for permanent settlements and farming. In some areas, most notably New England, the forests have been allowed to regenerate as the population moved west. The moisture of the area ensures that if cleared land is left alone, shrubs and small trees will quickly establish themselves, beginning the transformation back to forest.

Tony Chen and Linda Riebling, also of Springfield, Illinois, have planted their yard using alternatives to lawn grasses. Most of the plants are native to the area, including the ground cover with the heart-shaped leaves, violets (spp.), Turk's-cap lilies (*Lilium superbum*), and New England aster (*Aster novae-angliae*).
Chris Young photo

Oak, hickory, and maple are the predominant trees. Chestnuts, which were once numerous, have been almost wiped out by blight in the last hundred years. Forest plants include the shade-loving Jack-in-the-pulpit.

PLANT QUIRKS

Because the region is so diverse in exposure, temperature, soil type, and moisture, it is worth repeating: make sure you get to know every place in your yard where you wish to plant natives and to match the plants up with the exact conditions they need for optimum hardiness.

The plants of this region are for the most part, moisture lovers. In fact, some thrive in, on, or near ponds and streams. Bee balm, cardinal flower, hibiscus, Jack-in-the-pulpit, and cinnamon fern love these wet conditions. This region and the Coastal Plains are the best ecological bets for pond gardens because of their wet-loving plants and high rainfall.

Plants that like things drier and sunnier include bearberry and black-eyed Susans. Shade-loving ground covers that provide excellent lawn replacement include green-and-gold, and sedge grasses.

SITE PREPARATION

For best results eliminate existing vegetation by digging it up by hand to a depth sufficient to remove all roots, or by smothering it with newspapers (at least 10 sheets thick), or 12.5 centimetres (5 inches) of hardwood bark. Then add 20 centimetres (8 inches) of good topsoil containing micro-organisms and microrhiza (beneficial fungi) from a nursery. Make sure it is weed free!

Keep your eye and hand on any weeds that show up, so your plants will have all the room they need to spread and flourish.

Good air circulation with lots of room around each plant is essential in this moist region to prevent diseases and fungi.

It is a good idea to rake up and add leaf mulch and compost to take the place of forest leaves in providing a natural fertilizer and mulch. They will help the soil retain water and feed the millions of colonies of soil micro-organisms.

The soil is pretty acidic from all of those thousands of years of leaf mulch. Test your soil for nutrients and acidity, and try to find plants that suit your soil.

CLASSIC, AVAILABLE, "EASY-TO-GROWS"

LOW. Under 60 cm (24 in)

Wild Columbine (*Aquilegia canadensis*)
Zones 4–8. 30–37.5 cm (12–15 in)
Wiry stemmed, red tubular nodding
flowers with yellow centres
Perennial
Filtered shade, moderate water
Well-drained slightly acidic soil; from seed,
nursery seedlings
Attracts moths, hummingbirds, butterflies

Jack-In-The-Pulpit (*Arisaema triphyllum*)
Zones 4–9. 30–60 cm (12–24 in)
Large, long leaves, unique flower of sometimes
tipped, hooded pistil, red berries
Perennial
Shade, moderate–high water
Rich, moist, well-drained soil; as corms,
seedlings, bare root

Green-and-Gold (*Chrysogonum
virginianum* var. *virginianum*)
a.k.a. golden star
Zones 5–8. 10–30 cm (4–12 in), depending on
variety. "Allen Bush" is 20–30 cm (8–12 in);

"Springbrook" is 10 cm (4 in); *virginianum,
virginianum* is 20 cm (8 in)
Herbaceous (dies to ground level in winter)
Partial–full shade, moderate water
Moist–dry soil; from seedlings
Attracts butterflies and bees; excellent ground
cover of tightly formed green leaves topped with
golden-yellow daisylike flowers

Violets (*Viola* spp.)
Zones 4–10. 30 cm (12 in)
Five-petalled flowers, white, blue, deep purple,
yellow
Perennial
Full sun–filtered shade, moderate water
Rich soil; from seed, division
Attracts butterflies
Low-growing forms make a gorgeous ground
cover

Virginia Bluebells (*Mertensia virginica*)
Zones 3–9. 30–60 cm (12–24 in)
Lush green foliage, delicate, nodding blue bell-
shaped flowers
Perennial
Partial sun–shade, moderate water
Well-drained, fertile, moist soil; from seedlings
Buds start out pink, open to blue

Sweet William (*Phlox divaricata*)
a.k.a. woodland phlox, *P. canadensis*
Zones 3–9. 20–30 cm (8–12 in)
Excellent ground cover of medium–dark green
leaves, fragrant pastel blue flowers
Perennial
Partial sun–partial shade, moderate water
Fertile, organic soil; from seedlings, division
Attracts butterflies
My Mom's favourite; excellent ground cover

Celandine Poppy (*Stylophorum diphyllum*)
Zones 4–9. 30–75 cm (12–30 in)
Large deeply cut green leaves, large bright
yellow poppies
Perennial
Partial sun or shade, moderate water
Deep, organic soil; from seeds, seedlings
Attracts butterflies, bees, birds

Dwarf Crested Iris (*Iris cristata*)
Zones 3–9. 10–17.5 cm (4–7 in)
Light green grassy leaves, light to dark
blue/lavender or white flowers
Partial shade–light shade; moderate water
Well-drained soil; from seedlings,
rhizome division
Attracts birds, bees, butterflies
Spreads easily to make a great ground cover

MEDIUM: 60–180 cm (2–6 ft)

Carolina Phlox (*Phlox carolina*)
Zones 3–9. 30–120 cm (1–4 ft)
Deep green, glossy leaves, lavender,
pink flowers
Partial shade, moderate water
Fertile, organic soil; from seedlings, division
Attracts hummingbirds, butterflies

Bee Balm (*Monarda didyma*)
a.k.a. Oswego tea, oregano, etc.
Zones 4–9. 90–120 cm (3–4 ft)
Scarlet pom-pom-like flowers on stalks
emerging from large green leaves
Full sun, moderate–high water
Rich, moist soil; from seed, division
Attracts hummingbirds, bees, butterflies
Leaves edible as herbs

Black-eyed Susan (*Rudbeckia hirta*)
Zones 5–8. 90 cm (3 ft)
Annual, biennial, perennial

Yellow daisy with dark brown centres
on tall stalks, irislike leaves
Full sun, moderate–low water
Dry, acidic soil; from seed
Attracts butterflies
We grew up with this one!

Wild Blue Indigo
(*Baptisia australis* var. *australis*)
Zones 3–9. 90–120 cm (3–4 ft)
Shrubby light green foliage, foot-long stems
supporting indigo-blue flowers, coal coloured
seed pods
Perennial
Full sun–partial shade, low water
Fertile–poor soils; from seeds, seedlings, ball &
burlap, stem cuttings, 2- to 3-year-old plants
best for transplanting

Sundrops (*Oenothera fruticosa*)
Zones 4–9. 60–90 cm (2–3 ft)
Bright lemon-yellow flowers, deep green
leaves with maroon-red spots
Perennial
Full sun, low water
Well-drained, dry soils; from seed, seedlings
Attracts butterflies, birds, bees
An evening primrose; this one opens
in daylight

Kinnikinnick (*Arctostaphylos uva-ursi*)
a.k.a. bearberry
Zones 2–10. To 15 cm (6 in)
Evergreen
Trailing shrub, small leathery green leaves
turn bronze in winter, small white and pink
urn-shaped flowers, dark red berries
Full sun, low–moderate water
Dry, acidic, sandy soil; nursery seedlings
Attracts bears, deer, grouse, birds, butterflies
Be careful who you call to dinner!

New England Aster (*Aster novae-angliae*)
Zones 4–9. 180 cm (6 ft)
Perennial
Tall stems, narrow leaves, purple
daisylike flowers
Full sun, moderate water
Moist soil; from seed, division
Attracts butterflies, toads
Mow in early summer to keep its
compact size

Bayberry (*Myrica pensylvanica*)
Zones 2–7. 120 cm (4 ft)
Shrub of glossy green leaves that turn
red/bronze in winter, grey berries
Deciduous
Full sun, low water
Dry, sandy soil; from root cuttings, seedlings
Attracts tree swallows, other birds
Likes the dunes

TALL: 180 cm (6 ft) and over

Sourwood (*Oxydendrum arboreum*)
Zones 4–9. 12–15 m (30–50 ft)
Single trunk with lacy clusters of white beadlike
draping flowers, large glossy dark green leaves;
summer fruit opens to tan lace. Fall leaves are
red, burgundy, orange, purple
Sun or partial shade, low–moderate water
Prefers acidic, fertile, well-drained soil;
from seedlings, ball & burlap
Important honeybee tree

Eastern Redbud (*Cercis canadensis*)
a.k.a. Judas tree
Zones 4–9. 6–9 m (20–30 ft)
Dark green leaves with maroon tint,
heavy bloom of small bright rose to
lavender flowers
Deciduous
Full sun–partial shade; low water

Well-drained fertile soil; from seedlings,
ball & burlap
Attracts butterflies, blue jays
Member of the pea family, similar flowers

Sassafras (*Sassafras albidum*)
Zones 5–8. 18 m (60 ft)
Bright yellow-green flowers, red-orange leaves
in fall, green twigs in winter; deep blue fruit
Deciduous
Full sun, moderate water
Sandy, well-drained loam; difficult to transplant
if nursery seedling is large
Attracts birds and butterflies
One of the first trees to move into
unattended fields

Red-osier Dogwood (*Cornus sericea*)
Zones 4–9. 3 m (10 ft)
Shrub of bright red stems, clusters of cream
coloured flowers, white fruits
Full sun–partial shade, moderate–high water
Moist, acidic soil; from twigs, seedlings
Attracts rabbits, wood ducks and other
birds, butterflies
Beautiful all year round

Paper Birch (*Betula papyrifera*)
Zones 2–5. 24 m (80 ft)
Distinctive white peeling bark on mature
trees, pointed dark green leaves, yellow in fall
Deciduous
Full sun (north) partial sun (south);
moderate water
Well-drained sandy loam, ball & burlap
Attracts birds, butterflies
Used by first peoples for bark canoes,
teepee frames

Sugar Maple (*Acer saccharum*)
Zones 3–8. 27 m (90 ft)
Single trunk with large distinctive leaves that
turn gold, red, and yellow with the cold weather
Deciduous
Full sun–partial shade; moderate water
Well-drained moist soil; from seedlings,
ball & burlap
Attracts squirrels, birds, chipmunks
Sap is cooked for maple syrup

THE COASTAL PLAINS

The region extends 4,800 kilometres (3,000 miles)
along the Atlantic and Gulf Coasts, from
Massachusetts to Texas, then sends an arm north,
following the floodplain of the Mississippi River
into southern Illinois.

CLIMATE

The Coastal Plains are known for extremely hot,
humid weather and low-lying land. The habitat
varies greatly in this region, from salt and freshwater marshes, to dunes, to forests. The soil is var-
ied, ranging from pure sand at the shores to alkaline
clay in the "prairies," to acidic peat. If you live in
this region, you will need to plant natives that suit
the specific moisture and soil conditions of your
yard. A sandy beach exposed to salt, wind, and sun
will not sustain the same plants as a partially shad-
ed, moist, sandy loam.

PLANT HISTORY

There are bioregions within bioregions in this
Floristic Province, and plant species have evolved
according to the type of water (salt or fresh), soil
(dunes to prairie) and sun available to them. It is
essential that you plant according to the conditions
of your site, if your species are to thrive.

Top: This Alabama yard shows beautiful use of Coastal Plains Floristic Province native plants, and some non-natives, as well. The native alumroot (*Heuchera Americana*) forms a beautiful clump of upright stalks with tiny flowers, while sweet William (*Phlox divaricata*) and foamflower (*Tiarella cordifolia* var. *collina*) grow out of a matrix of native mosses and ferns. *Andy Wasowski photo*

Bottom: This was once a turf-grass lawn, until the owner allowed nature to take its course. The velvety fern moss (*Thuidium delicatulum*) found the acidity of the soil, shade and natural moisture perfectly to its liking and gradually overtook the struggling grass. The volunteer flowers that show up from time to time in the moss are mowed once a year. *Andy Wasowski photo*

Before contact, first peoples had a veritable Garden of Eden at their "doorsteps": salt and freshwater fish, edible plants, and wildlife. Since contact, the landscape has changed. Huge cotton plantations exhausted the soils, and exotic gardens were a sign of refinement and wealth. Thankfully, many southerners knew a good thing when they saw it, and have continued to plant with the native beauties of this region.

Dune species include grasses such as American beach grass and sea oats. Accents of brilliant colour can be added by planting the gorgeous blanket flower variety that is native here. Needle rush, switch grass, and groundsel tree do well at salt-marsh edges. Shrubs that can withstand the salt spray include wax myrtle and bayberry.

Farther inland, the well-drained soils of the barrier islands provide a maritime forest with live oak, red cedar, southern magnolia and flowering dogwood.

Freshwater gardening has evolved an entirely different set of species. White-flowered water lilies, yellow American lotus, and floating heart are all freshwater pond dwellers. The blue flag iris, wild red mallow, and swamp rose love freshwater marsh land. Bald cypress, water tupelo, swamp gum, red maple, and swamp dogwood all do well in low-lying woods close to streams.

The Flatwoods region produces sweet bay, summersweet, and azaleas.

The Coastal Plains "prairie" has a population of grasses that grow in the Great Plains, including big bluestem, little bluestem, and Indian grass. Purple coneflower and blazing star grow here as well.

Golden aster, sandhill lupine, red basil, and sparkleberry are a few of the plants that grow in the sand hill habitats of the Coastal Plains. These hills or ridges have been formed by sand that has been deposited by river water.

The southern hardwood forest is known for its magnolia trees, American beech, and buckeyes.

PLANT QUIRKS

The plants of this region must be able to withstand high humidity in all seasons. This is one of the few regions where I personally would recommend a pond garden, because rainfall is sufficient to keep it fed, and many of the native plants like damp feet.

SITE PREPARATION

Little preparation is needed, except the usual digging out or smothering of non-native species before you start, and planning ahead so that each plant goes in its optimum place in the garden. Also, of course, compost your kitchen waste and add it to your soil.

CLASSIC, AVAILABLE, "EASY-TO-GROWS"

LOW: Under 60 cm (24 in)

Stokes Aster (*Stokesia laevis*)
Zones 5–10. 30–60 cm (12–24 in)
Leafy stems with up to 7 large powder blue
flower heads, basal leaves evergreen
Evergreen perennial
Full sun–partial shade, low water
Dry, poor soil; from seeds, seedlings, division
Hardy native from South Carolina to Louisiana

Blanket Flower (*Gaillardia pulchella*)
a.k.a. fire wheels, Indian blanket
Zones 5–9. 30–60 cm (12–24 in)
Reddish brown–yellow or purple ray flowers
tipped with bright yellow
Perennial on Gulf Coast
Full sun, low water, salt/wind tolerant
Sandy soil; from seeds, seedlings

Carolina Phlox (*Phlox carolina*)
Zones 7–9. 30–90 cm (2–3 ft)
Clusters of pink-purple flowers, dark green
foliage
Perennial
Partial sun or shade, moderate water
Prefers fertile, organic soil; will tolerate
dry soil; from seed

Dwarf Crested Iris (*Iris cristata*)
Zones 4–9. 10–17.5 cm (4–7 in)
Swordlike leaves, flaglike flowers lavender-
blue with yellow crest, faintly fragrant
Partial shade, moderate water
Well-drained soil; from rhizomes,
seedlings, division
Excellent ground cover, spreads to form wide
clumps

Green-and-Gold
(*Chrysogonum virginianum* var. *australis*)
Zones 7–8. 5–10 cm (2–4 in)
Tightly formed green hairy leaves topped with
bright golden-yellow sunflower like flowers
Herbaceous perennial
Partial shade, low water
Well-drained poor soil; from seedlings, division
One of the best ground covers for this region

Rose Verbena (*Verbena canadensis*)
Zones 7–11. 20–45 cm (8–18 in)
Deep lobed leaves, showy clusters of
small tubular red–pink flowers
Herbaceous perennial
Full sun, low water
Most soils; from seedlings, stems root
where they touch the ground
Attracts butterflies, birds, bees
Excellent ground cover, the plants form
dense mats

Wild Ginger (*Asarum canadense*)
Zones 7–8. 15–20 cm (6–8 in)
Heart-shaped aromatic leaves, 2.5 cm-wide
bell-shaped flowers, purple green on
outside, deep maroon inside
Herbaceous perennial
Shade, moderate–high water
Humus soil; from rhizomes, seedlings
Attracts butterflies, bees
Another excellent lawn replacement!

Wood Fern (*Dryopteris marginalis*)
Zones 5–8. 60 cm (24 in)
Clump-forming upright fern with
delicately shaped fronds
Evergreen
Shade, moderate water
Well-drained soil with lots of organic
matter; from seedlings
Will tolerate drought if in shade

MEDIUM: 60–180 cm (2–6 ft)

Summersweet (*Clethra alnifolia*)
a.k.a. sweet pepperbush
Zones 5–9. To 180 cm (6 ft)
Glossy green leaves, long clusters of
fragrant white or pink flowers
Deciduous shrub
Sun or partial shade, high water
Moist, poorly drained, acidic soils;
from seedlings, cuttings
Attracts birds, butterflies
Excellent for damp areas, tolerates heat
and seaside conditions

Swamp Azalea (*Rhododendron viscosum*)
Zones 3–9. 90–45 cm (3–15 ft)
Fragrant white, pink, clusters of funnel-shaped
flowers, glossy rounded deep-green leaves
Deciduous shrub
Light shade, moderate water
Acidic, well-drained soil; from seedlings,
ball & burlap
Attracts butterflies, birds
One of the hardiest, makes a good shrub border
when planted 120 cm (4 ft) apart

Southern Blue Flag (*Iris virginica*)
Zones 3–7. 90 cm (3 ft)
Lavender or blue flowers, waxy green leaves
Perennial
Full sun, high water, likes swamps, bogs or
water gardens
Fertile, organic, wet soil; from seedlings, bare root

Oakleaf Hydrangea (*Hydrangea quercifolia*)
Coastal Plains native. 120–180 cm (4–6 ft)
Hairy reddish twigs, large oak-shaped leaves,
large showy clusters of white flowers that turn
pink later in summer
Deciduous shrub
Full sun–partial shade, moderate water
Rich, well-drained, moist soil; from seedlings
Attracts butterflies

Carolina Jessamine (*Gelsemium sempervirens*)
a.k.a. Carolina jasmine, yellow jasmine
Zone 9. 3–6 m (10–20 ft)
Evergreen vine, shiny green leaves, clusters of
fragrant, bright yellow funnel-shaped flowers
Full sun–light shade, low–moderate water
Fertile, well-drained soil; from seedlings, cuttings
Attracts birds, butterflies
State flower of South Carolina. Can be planted
90 cm (3 ft) apart and trailed across the yard as
a ground cover, or up a trellis or mailbox

TALL: 180 cm (6 ft) and over

Hoary Azalea
(*Rhododendron canescens*)
a.k.a. Piedmont or Florida Pinxter
Zones 5–9. 3–4.5 m (10–15 ft)
Large upright shrub with pink tubular
blossoms, light green leaves
Deciduous
Full sun–part shade, moderate water
Moist, well-drained soil; by seed, cuttings,
seedlings
Attracts butterflies

Silverbell (*Halesia carolina*)
a.k.a. silverbell tree, snowdrop tree
Zones 4–8. 9–12 m (30–40 ft)
Green leaves turn yellow in fall. Many clusters
of drooping, bell-shaped white blossoms
Deciduous tree
Partial shade, moderate water
Well-drained acidic soil; from seedlings
Attracts birds, butterflies
Excellent natural pest resistance

Wax Myrtle (*Myrica cerifera*)
Zones 6–9. 9 m (30 ft)
Shrub of fine-textured pale green linear leaves,
fragrant when crushed; tiny grey fruits in fall
Evergreen
Sun–partial shade, low water; tolerates salt
spray and wind
Poor soil; from seedlings
Attracts birds

American Holly (*Ilex opaca*)
Zones 5–9. 4.5–9 m (15–30 ft) in garden
Cut-out glossy green leaves, bright red berries
Evergreen
Full sun–partial shade, moderate water
Well-drained acidic soil; from cuttings, seedlings
Attracts birds, butterflies

Flowering Dogwood (*Cornus florida*)
Zones 5–9. 6 m (20 ft)
Extensive branches covered in white flowers, leaves turn purple-red in fall, glossy red fruit
Deciduous
Full sun–partial shade, moderate water
Well-drained, acidic, moist soil; from seed, seedling, cuttings
Attracts birds, butterflies

Sour Gum (*Nyssa sylvatica*)
a.k.a. black gum
Zones 4–9. 9–15 m (30–50 ft)
Pyramid-shaped leaf mass, thick, shiny green in summer, brilliant reds, oranges and golds in fall, red buds in spring; dark blue fruits in fall
Deciduous
Full sun–partial shade; moderate water
Well-drained moist soil; difficult to transplant due to deep taproot, from ball & burlap in spring
Attracts birds

Coral Honeysuckle (*Lonicera sempervirens*)
Zones 6–9. 3–6 m (10–20 ft)
Twining, climbing vine, deep green leaves, coral coloured flowers with yellow insides are trumpet-shaped, red fruits in summer
Deciduous
Full sun–partial shade; moderate water
Well-drained moist soil; from cuttings, seed, seedlings
Attracts butterflies, hummingbirds and others

Southern Magnolia (*Magnolia grandiflora*)
Zones 7–9. 18 m (60 ft)
Large dark green leathery leaves, rust undersides, huge fragrant white flowers, reddish-brown fruits
Evergreen
Full sun–partial shade; moderate water
Fertile soil; from seedlings, ball & burlap
Attracts just about everything!

Resources, Contacts, Supplies

(by Floristic Province)

Note: I have tried to list the Native Plant Societies and other organizations that can give you information at the beginning of each section. This is followed by arboreta, botanic gardens, and finally, private nurseries.

This is a list, not an endorsement of any nursery. Many native plant societies have local chapters within their states or provinces. Check them out! They will also have up-to-date information on other plant sources.

CALIFORNIA
FLORISTIC PROVINCE

STATEWIDE

California Native Plant Society
Suite 17, 1722 J St
Sacramento, CA 95814-2931
(916) 447-2677
cnps@cnps.org
www.cnps.org

Growing Native Newsletter
PO Box 489
Berkeley, CA 94701
(510) 232-9865
ladylfab@earthlink.net
www.growingnative.com

NORTH

Bitterroot Restoration Inc
Suite 5, 11760 Atwood Rd
Auburn, CA 95603
(530) 745-9814
laurie@bitterrootrestoration.com

Paul Furman
Edgehill Mountain Open Space Park
San Francisco, CA 94114

(415) 865-0324
paul@edgehill.net
www.edgehill.net

Go Native Nursery
333 Cypress St
Moss Beach, CA 94038
(650) 728-0728
gonative@coastside.net
www.gonativenursery.com

Larner Seeds
PO Box 407
Bolinas, CA 94924
(415) 868-9407
info@larnerseeds.com

Yerba Buena Nursery
19500 Skyline Blvd
Woodside, CA 94062
(650) 851-1668
www.yerbabuenanursery.com

Freshwater Farms Inc
5851 Myrtle Ave
Eureka, CA 95503-9510
(707) 444-8261 or (800) 200-8969
www.freshwaterfarms.com

CENTRAL

Santa Barbara Botanic Garden
1212 Mission Canyon Rd
Santa Barbara, CA 93105
(805) 682-4726

Las Pilitas Nursery
3232 Las Pilitas Rd
Santa Margarita, CA 93453
(805) 438-5992
www.laspilitas.com

Las Pilitis Nursery
8331 Nelson Way at Old Hwy 395
Escondido, CA 92026
(760) 822-1350
www.laspilitas.com

Native Sons Nursery
379 W El Campo Rd
Arroyo Grande, CA 93420
(805) 481-5996
www.nativeson.com

SOUTH

The Living Desert Public Garden
47900 South Portola Ave
Palm Desert, CA 92260
(760) 346-5694
www.desertusa.com

S & S Seeds
5690 Casitas Path Rd
Carpinteria, CA 93013
(805) 484-0551 or
(800) 423-8112 in CA
www.ssseeds.com

Bitterroot Restoration
Suite 117E, 3702 Via De La Ville
Del Mar, CA 92014
(858) 481-5865
dug@bitterrootrestoration.com

Theodore Payne Foundation
10459 Tuxford St
Sun Valley, CA 91352
(818) 768-1802
www.theodorepayne.org

Mostly Natives Nursery
27235 Highway One
Tomales, CA 94971
(707) 878-2009
www.mostlynatives.com

PACIFIC NORTHWEST FLORISTIC PROVINCE

BRITISH COLUMBIA: Western

Native Plant Society of
British Columbia
2012 William St
Vancouver, BC V5L 2X6
(604) 792-1891
npsbc@hotmail.com

Garry Oak Meadow
Preservation Society
A-954 Queens Avenue
Victoria, BC V8T 1M6
(250) 475-2024
garry1oak@netscape.net

Victoria Horticultural Society
Native Plant Study Group
PO Box 5081, Stn B
Victoria, BC V8R 6N9
(250) 592-8618

Alba Landscape Consultants
2224 Mills Rd
Sidney, BC V8L 2C1
(250) 656-8812
gordon_mackay@yahoo.com

Naturescape BC
Box 9354, Stn. Prov. Gov.
Victoria, BC V8W 9M1
(800) 387-9853
www.hctf.ca/nature.htm

Wildlife Habitat
Demonstration Garden
5216 Glencairn Dr
Burnaby, BC V5B 3C1
(604) 526-7275
www.wildliferescue.ca

North Vancouver City Hall
141 West 14th St
North Vancouver, BC V7M 1H9
Contact: Dave Hutch
(604) 985-7761, ext 394
dhutch@cnv.org

UBC Botanical Garden
6804 SW Marine Dr
Vancouver, BC V6T 1Z4
(604) 822-9666, (604) 822-4208
www.ubcbotanicalgarden.org

BC's Wild Heritage Plants
47330 Extrom Rd
Chilliwack, BC V2R 4V1
(604) 858-5141
bcwild@uniserve.com

Fraser's Thimble Farms
175 Arbutus Rd
Salt Spring Island, BC V8K 1A3
(250) 537-5788
www.thimblefarms.ca

Pacific Rim Native Plants Nursery
44305 Old Orchard Rd
Chilliwack, BC V2R 1A9
(604) 792-9279
www.hillkeep.ca
paige@hillkeep.ca

Streamside Native Plants
3222 Grant Rd
RR 6, Site 695, C6
Courtenay, BC V9N 8H9
(250) 338-7509
www.streamsidenativeplants

Madrone Wildlife Gardens
1877 Herd Rd
Duncan, BC V9L 5W4
(250) 746-0115
madrocon@cowichan.com

NATS Nursery Ltd
17127 Fraser Hwy
Surrey, BC V3S 4R5
(604) 576-1300
nats@bcnta.nwave.com
www.nats-nursery.com

Van Dusen Botanical Garden
5251 Oak St
Vancouver, BC V6M 4H1
(604) 878- 9274
carolyn_jones@city.vancouver.bc.ca
(250) 498-8898

Fragrant Flora
RR 22, 3741 Sunshine Coast Hwy
Roberts Creek, BC V0N 2W2
(604) 885-6142
fragrantflora@sunshine.net

WASHINGTON STATE

Washington Native Plant Society
7400 Sand Point Way NE
Seattle, WA 98115
(206) 527-3210
(888) 288-8022
www.wnps.org

NatureScaping Wildlife
Botanical Gardens
11000 NE 149th St
Vancouver, WA 98682
fax: (360) 604-4400

Abundant Life Seed Foundation
Box 772, 930 Lawrence St
Port Townsend, WA 98368
(360) 385-5660
www.abundantlifeseed.org

Barford's Hardy Ferns
23622 Bothell Way
Bothell, WA 98021
(206) 483-0205

Black Lake Organic Nursery and
Garden Store
4711 Black Lake Blvd
Olympia, WA 98512
(360) 786-0537
www.blacklakeorganic.com

Cloud Mountain Farm
6906 Goodwin Rd
Everson, WA 98247
(360) 966-5859
www.cloudmountainfarm.com

Forest Floor Recovery
Nursery and Floral
PO Box 89
Lummi Island, WA 98262
(360) 758-2778
ffrn1234@aol.com

Northwest Nurseries Inc
8818 132nd Ave NE
Redmond, WA 98052
(425) 822-0076
Nnurseries@aol.com

Native Origins Nursery
1129 Water St
Raymond, WA 98577
(360) 942-0027
maryann@willapabay.org

OREGON

Native Plant Society of Oregon
PO Box 902
Eugene, OR 97440
www.NPSOregon.org

Berry Botanic Garden
11505 SW Summerville Ave
Portland, OR 97219
(503) 636-4112
www.berrybot.org

Siskiyou Rare Plant Nursery
2825 Cummings Rd
Medford, OR 97501
(541) 772-6846
www.srpn.net

Silver Springs Nursery
3400 Little Applegate Rd
Jacksonville, OR 97530
Trade wholesale only
(541) 899-1065

Leach Botanical Garden
6704 SE 122nd Ave
Portland, OR 97236
(503) 823-9503
www.portlandparks.org

AlderView Natives
28315 SW Grahams Ferry Rd
Wilsonville, OR 97070
(503) 570-2894
natives1@gte.net

Balance Restoration Nursery
27995 Chambers Mill Rd
Lorane, OR 97451
(541) 942-5530
tamfrobinson@cs.com

Curry Native Plants
92545 Silver Butte Rd
Port Orford, OR 97465
Dale Lee
(541) 332-5635
daleleenews@hotmail.com

Northwest Native Plants Inc
23501 Beatie Rd
Oregon City, OR 97045
(503) 632-7079
nwnative@bctonline.com

Freshwater Farms/North Coast
Native Seed Bank
5851 Myrtle Ave
Eureka, CA 95503-9510
(707) 444-8261
(800) 200-8969
r.store@worldnet.att.net
www.freshwaterfarms.com

SOUTHWESTERN DESERTS FLORISTIC PROVINCE

NEVADA: Southern

Mojave Native Plant Society
8180 Placid Dr
Las Vegas, NV 89123

Desert Demonstration Garden
3701 W Alta Dr
Las Vegas, NV 89153
(702) 258-3205

Ethel M Botanic Garden
2 Cactus Garden Dr
Henderson, NV 89014
(702) 542-0713
www.ethelm.com

University of Nevada Las Vegas
Arboretum
4505 Maryland Pkwy
Las Vegas, NV 89154
(702) 739-3392

NEW MEXICO: Southwest

Native Plant Society of New Mexico
734 North Reymont St
Las Cruces, NM 88002
chapter contact: Lisa Mandelkern
(505) 526-0917
www.npsnm.unm.edu

Enchanted Gardens
413 W Griggs Ave
Las Cruces, NM 88005
(505) 524-1886
www.nmenchantedgardens.com

ARIZONA: Southwest

Arizona Native Plant Society
PO Box 41206, Sun Station
Tuscon, AZ 85717
askplants@AZNPS.org
www.aznps.org

Arizona-Sonora Desert Museum
2021 N Kinney Rd
Tucson, AZ 85743
(520) 883-1380

Arizona Botanical Gardens
1601 W Hwy 89A
Clarkdale, AZ 86324
(928) 634-2166

Boyce-Thompson Arboretum
37615 U.S. Highway 60
Superior, AZ 85273
(520) 689-2723

Desert Botanical Garden
1201 N. Galvin Parkway

Phoenix, AZ 85008
(480) 941-1217

Tohono Chul Park
7366 N Paseo del Norte
Tuscon, AZ 85704
(520) 742-6455
www.tohonochulpark.org

Ahakhav Native Plant Nursery
Rte 1, Box 23 B
Parker, AZ 85344
(928) 669-2664
www.ahakhav.com

American Desert Plants
4729 N Silverbell
Tucson, AZ 85745
(520) 792-2041
cactus@desertplants.com

Planting Eden Native Nursery
HC 68 Box 2122
Kirkland, AZ 86332
(520) 427-9457
by appointment only
plantingeden@W3az.net

The Garden Gate
11416 E Desert Cove
Scottsdale, AZ 85259
(480) 661-8077

TEXAS: Southwest

Native Plant Society of Texas
Suite 3, 117 W 7th St
Georgetown, TX 78626-0891
(512) 868-8799
www.npsot.org

Chihuahuan Desert Research
Institute
PO Box 905
Fort Davis, TX 79734
(915) 364-2499

El Paso Native Plant Society
7760 Maya Ave
El Paso, TX 79931

WESTERN MOUNTAINS AND BASINS FLORISTIC PROVINCE

BRITISH COLUMBIA: Central/Eastern

Xeriscape Demonstration Garden
McArthur Island
contact: Diane Hale
Utilities Engineer
City of Kamloops Engineering Dept
7 Victoria St W
Kamloops, BC V2C 1A2
(250) 828-3461

Bluestem Nursery & Ornamental
Grasses
1946 Fife Rd
Christina Lake, BC V0H 1E3
(250) 447-6363

Sagebrush Native Plant Nursery
38206 93rd St
RR 2, Site 13, C 10,
Oliver, BC V0H 1T0
(250) 498-8898

Dry Valley Gardens
667 Curtis Rd
Kelowna, BC V1V 2C9
(250) 762-6018
dryvalley@look.ca

Okanogan Native Habitats
825 de Hart Rd
Kelowna, BC V1W 4N2
(250) 764-8899

ALBERTA: Southwest

Alberta Native Plant Council
Box 52099, Garneau Postal Outlet
Edmonton, AB T6G 2T5
www.anpc.ab.ca

Naturescape Alberta
Box 785
Red Deer, AB T4N 5H2
www.naturescape.ab.ca

Alberta Nurseries & Seeds
Box 20

Bowden, AB T0M 0K0
(403) 224-3545
dectod@telusplanet.net
www.gardenersweb.com

Bearberry Creek Greenhouses
RR 2
Sundre, AB T0M 1X0
(403) 638-4231

Bow Point Nursery
244034 Range Rd 32
Calgary, AB T3E 6W3
(403) 686-4434
bowpoint@agt.net

Eagle Lake Nurseries
Box 2340
Strathmore, AB T1P 1K3
(403) 934-3622
eglake@telusplanet.net

Enviroscapes
Box 38
Warner, AB T0K 2L0
(403) 733-2160
enscapes@telusplanet.net

WASHINGTON: Central/Eastern

Washington Native Plant Society
Okanogan Chapter
PO Box 892
Winthrop, WA 98862
(509) 996-3458
bearfight@methow.com

Washington Native Plant Society
Wenatchee Chapter
L. Malmquist
3352 Hansel Lane
Peshastin, WA 98847-9419

Rain Shadow Nursery
641 Camion Rd
Ellensburg, WA 98926
(509) 968-4778
rainshdw@sisna.com

Methow Natives
19 Aspen Lane
Winthrop, WA 98862
(509) 966-3562

methownatives@methow.com
www.methow.com/~mnatives/

Plants of the Wild
PO Box 866
123 Stateline Rd
Tekoa, WA 99033
(509) 284-2848
www.plantsofthewild.com

Inland Native Plant Producers
WSU/Spokane County Cooperative
Extension
222 N. Havana St
Spokane, WA 99202
Contact: Tonie Fitzerald
(509) 477-2164

Wildlands Inc
1941 Saint St
Richland, WA 99352
(509) 375-4177
wildland@gte.net

Garden Gate Growers
38 Mink Creek Rd
Kettle Falls, WA 99141
(509) 738-4456
tlkowitz@yahoo.com

Rainier Seed Inc
1404 4th St
PO Box 1064
Davenport, WA 99122
(509) 725-1235
hwood@rainierseeds.com

Sun Mountain Native Seed
Suite 400, N 120 Wall
Spokane, WA 99201
(509) 835-4967
mark@landmarkseed.com
www.sunmountainseeds.com

Prairie Bloom Nursery
5602 State Rte 270
Pullman, WA 99163
(509) 332-4425

OREGON: Central/Eastern

Native Plant Society of Oregon
PO Box 902
Eugene, OR 97440
www.NPSOregon.org

CALIFORNIA: Northeast

California Native Plant Society
Shasta Chapter
Don Burk
www.snowcrest.net.cnp
burk@c-zone.net

NEVADA: Northern

Northern Nevada Native Plant
Society
PO Box 8965
Reno, NV 89507-8965
(775) 668-1180
www.state.nv.us/nvnhp/nnnps.htm
jsawasaki@hotmail.com

ARIZONA: Northeast

Arizona Native Plant Society
PO Box 41206, Sun Station
Tuscon, AZ 85717-1206
askplants@AZNPS.org
www.aznps.org

The Arboretum at Flagstaff
4001 Woody Mountain Rd
Flagstaff, AZ 86001
(928) 774-1442
www.thearb.org

Flagstaff Native Plant and Seed
400 E. Butler Ave
Flagstaff, AZ 86001
(928) 773-940
info@flnativeplant.com

UTAH

Utah Native Plant Society
PO Box 520041
Salt Lake City, UT 84152-0041
(801) 272-3275
www.unps.org

Wildland Nursery
550 North Hwy 89
Joseph, UT 84739
(435) 527-1234
www.wildlandnursery.com

Great Basin Natives
75 West 300 S
Holden, UT 84636
(435) 795-2303
www.grownative.com

High Desert Gardens
2971 S Hwy 191
Moab, UT 84532
(435) 259-4531

Utah Wildflower Seeds
PO Box 2114
Hilldale, UT 84784
(801) 972-3910
www.wildflowersunlimited.com

Utah Native Seeds
PO Box 355
Eureka, UT 84628
(435) 433-6924

Granite Seed Co
1697 W 2100 N
Lehi, UT 84043
(801) 768-4422
granite@graniteseed.com
www.graniteseed.com

Lone Peak State Conservation
Nursery
271 West Bitterbrush Lane
Draper, UT 84020-9599
(801) 571-0900
www.lnr.state.ut.us/flf/lonepeak/
home2.htm

IDAHO

Idaho Native Plant Society
PO Box 9451
Boise, ID 83707-3451
www.idahonativeplants.org
idnativeplants@sixone.com

Idaho Botanical Garden
2355 N Penitentiary Rd
Boise, ID 83712
(208) 343-8649

Northplan/Mountain Seed
PO Box 9107
Moscow, ID 83843-1607
(208) 822-8040

Wildlife Habitat Institute
1025 E Hatter Creek Rd
Princeton, ID 83857
(208) 587-2500
wild@potlatch.com

Bonners Ferry Nursery
HCR 85 Box 336
Bonners Ferry, ID 83805
(208) 267-3020
fax: (208) 267-4015
bfntrees@coldreams.net
www.kvng.com

Buffalo Berry Farm
51 East Lake Fort Rd
McCall, ID 83638
fax: (208) 634-3062

BNB Nursery Inc
BCR 62 Box 108
Moyie Springs, ID 83845
(208) 267-4501

Clifty View Nursery
Rte 1, Box 509
Bonners Ferry, ID 83805
(208) 267-7129
www.cliftyview.com

Hash Tree Co
1199 Bear Creek Rd
Princeton, ID 83857
(208) 267-5753
sales@hashtree.com
www.hashtree.com

Silver Springs Nursery
PO Box 355
Moyie Springs, ID 83845
(208) 267-5733
ssninc@coldreams.com

MONTANA: Western

Montana Native Plant Society
PO Box 8783
Missoula, MT 59807-8783

Montana State University Arboretum
W College Ave & S 11th Ave
Bozeman, MT 59717
www.gardenguide.montana.edu

Lawyer Nursery
950 Hwy 200 W
Plains, MT 59859
(406) 826-3881

Valley Nursery
PO Box 4845
2801 N Montana Ave
Helena, MT 59604

WYOMING: Western

Wyoming Native Plant Society
Suite 2, 1604 Grand Ave
Laramie, WY 82070
www.rmh.uwyo.edu/wnps.html

COLORADO: Western

Colorado Native Plant Society
PO Box 200
Fort Collins, CO 80522-0200
(303) 443-9365
www.conps.org

City of Boulder Open Spaces
PO Box 791
Boulder, CO 80306
(720) 564-2057
www.ci.boulder.co.us/openspace/
nature/gardens/gardens/htm
sutherlandD@ci.boulder.co.us

Denver Botanic Garden
1005 York St
Denver, CO 80206
(720) 865-3500

Oxley Homestead
24425 W Currant Dr
Golden, CO 80401
(303) 526-9463

Western Native Seed
PO Box 188
Coaldale, CO 81222
(719) 942-3935
www.westernnativeseed.com
westseed@chaffee.net

Chelsea Nursery
3347 G Rd
Clifton, CO 81520
(970) 434-8434

Camelot Gardens
16612 Hwy 550
Montrose, CO 81401
(970) 249-6190

Beauty Beyond Belief
Wildflower Seed Co
#104, 3307 S College
Fort Collins, CO 80525
(970) 204-0596

Sage Garden
1207 2490 Lane
Hotchkiss, CO 81419
(970) 835-8805

Rocky Mountain Seed Co
1325 15th St
Denver, CO 80202
(303) 623-6223

Rocky Mountain Native Plants Co
3780 Silt Mesa Rd
Rifle, CO 81650
(970) 625-4769

Pawnee Buttes Seed Inc
PO Box 100
Greeley, CO 80632
(970) 356-7002
pawneeseed@ctos.com
www.pawneebuttesseed.com

NEW MEXICO: Upper west

Native Plant Society of New Mexico
PO Box 5917
Sante Fe, NM 87502-5917
www.npsnm.unm.edu

Living Desert Zoo and Garden
1504 Miehls Dr
Carlsbad, NM 88220
(505) 887-5516

Agua Fria Nursery
1409 Agua Fria St
Santa Fe, NM 87505
(505) 983-4831

Bernardo Beach Native Plant Farm
520 Montano Road NW
Albuquerque, NM 87107
(505) 345-6248

Desert Moon Nursery
PO Box 600
Veguita, NM 87062
(505) 864-0614

Plants of the Southwest
930 Baca St
Santa Fe, NM 87501
(505) 983-1548

Go Native!
New Mexico
(800) 880-4698
gonative@webcom.com

Albuquerque Xeriscape Garden
Osuna & Wyoming, NE
Albuquerque, NM 87197
(505) 857-8650

Bosque del Apache National
Wildlife Refuge
PO Box 1246
1001 Hwy 1
San Antonio, NM 87832
(505) 835-1828
fax: (505) 835-0314

GREAT PLAINS
FLORISTIC PROVINCE

ALBERTA: Southeast

Alberta Native Plant Council
Box 52099, Garneau Postal Outlet
Edmonton, AB T6G 2T5

(780) 427-5209
www.anpc.ab.ca

Devonian Botanic Garden
University of Alberta
Edmonton, AB T6G 2E1
(780) 987-3054
idymock@gpu.srv.ualberta.ca
www.discoveredmonton.com/
devonian

Bedrock Seed Bank
Box 54044
Forest Hts Stn
Edmonton, AB T6A 3Y7
(780) 992-9430
bedrock@theoffice.net
www.bedrockseedbank.com

Prairie Seeds Inc
1805-8 St
Nisku, AB T9E 7S8
(800) 222-6443
www.prairieseeds.com

SASKATCHEWAN: Southern

Blazing Star Wildflower Seed Co
Box 143 St
Benedict, SK S0K 3T0
(306) 289-2046
www.melford.com/wildflower

Prairiescape
2815 Pasqua St
Regina, SK S4S 2H4
(306) 586-6576
prairie@accesscomm.ca

MANITOBA: Southern

Living Prairie Museum
prairiem@city.winnipeg.mb.ca

Boughen Nurseries
PO Box 12
Valley River, MB R0L 2B0
(204) 638-7618

Prairie Originals
17 Schreyer Cr
St. Andrews, MB R1A 3A6

(204) 338-7517
prairieo@mbsympatico-ca

Prairie Habitats
PO Box 10
Argyle, MB R0C 0B0
(204) 467-9371
www.prairiehabitats.com

MONTANA: Eastern

Montana Native Plant Society
PO Box 8783
Missoula, MT 59807-8782

WYOMING: Eastern

Wyoming Native Plant Society
PO Box 3452
Laramie, WY 82071
www.rmh.uwyo.edu/wnps.html
clyde@uwyo.edu

COLORADO: Eastern

American Penstemon Society
1569 South Holland Ct
Lakewood, CO 80226

Colorado Native Plant Society
PO Box 200
Fort Collins, CO 80522-0200
www.conps.org

NEW MEXICO: Eastern

Native Plant Society of New Mexico
734 North Reymont St
Las Cruces, NM 88022

Living Desert Zoo and Gardens
1504 Miehls Dr
Carlsbad, NM 88220
(505) 887-5516
www.livingdesert@caverns.com

TEXAS: North/Central

Lady Bird Johnson
Wildflower Center
4801 LaCrosse Blvd
Austin, TX 78739-1702
(512) 292-4200
www.wildflower.org

Natives of Texas
6520 Medina Hwy
Kerrville, TX 78028
(830) 896-2169
bettyw@ktc.co

Rohde's Nursery
1651 Wall St
Garland, TX 75041
(972) 864-1934
grhode@aol.com
www.beorganic.com

Sweet Briar Nursery & Gardens
13999 FM 2305
Belton, TX 76513
(254) 780-4233

Wildseed Inc
PO Box 308
1101 Campo Rosa Rd
Eagle Lake, TX 77434
(800) 222-0156

Turner Seed Co
211 CR 151
Breckenridge, TX 76424
(254) 559-2065

Antique Rose Emporium
Rte 5, Box 143
9300 Lueckemeyer Rd
Brenham, TX 77833
(979) 836-9051

Bolton Works Nursery
333 W Hwy 290
PO Box 1100
Dripping Springs, TX 78620
(512) 894-4234
dnorman@wimberley-tx.com

San Antonio Botanical Garden
555 Funston Pl
San Antonio, TX 78209
(210) 207-3250

Dallas Arboretum &
Botanical Garden
8525 Garland Rd
Dallas, TX 74218
(214) 327-8263

OKLAHOMA

Oklahoma Native Plant Society
Tulsa Garden Center
2435 S. Peoria
Tulsa, OK 74114-1350

KANSAS

Kansas Wildflower Society
c/o R.L. McGregor Herbarium
U. of Kansas
2045 Constant Ave
Lawrence, KS 66047-3729
c-freeman@ukans.edu

Cimarron National Grasslands
242 East Hwy 56
Elkhart, KS 67950
(620) 697-4621

Dyck Arboretum of the Plains
Hesston College
177 W. Hickory
Hesston, KS 67062
(620) 327-8127
www.hesston.edu/arbor
arboretum@hesston.edu

NEBRASKA

Prairie/Plains Resource Institute
1307 L Street
Aurora, NE 68818
(402) 694-5535

Bluebird Nursery/Garden Land
521 Linden St
Clarkson, NE 68629
(402) 892-3442

Homestead National Monument
8523 W. State Hwy 4
Beatrice, NE 68310
(402) 223-3514
www.nps.gove/home

Stock Seed Farms Inc
28008 Mill Rd
Murdock, NE 68407
(402) 867-3771
(800) 759-1520

www.stockseed.com
stockseed@alltel.net

DAKOTAS

Great Plains Native Plant Society
Cindy Reed
PO Box 461
Hot Springs, SD 57747-0461
cascade@gwtc.net

Renewable Resources, LLC
20471 436th Ave
DeSmet, SD 57231
(605) 854-3971
rcp1@dtgnet.com
www.renewableresourcesllc.com

Gunlogson Nature Preserve
Icelandic State Park
13571 Hwy 5 West
Cavalier, ND 58220
(701) 265-4561

MINNESOTA

Applied Ecology: Native Landscape
Restoration & Management
4316-45th Ave S
Minneapolis, MN 55406
(612) 724-8916

Carlson Prairie Seed Farm
13071 260th St NW
Newfolden, MN 56738
(218) 523-5072

Prairie Restorations
PO Box 327
Princeton, MN 55371
(763) 631-9458

Minnesota Native Plant Society
220 Bio Sci Center
U. of Minnesota
1445 Gortner Ave
St Paul, MN 55108-1020
www.stolaf.edu/depts/biology/mnps
david.Johnson@usfamily.net

Feder's Prairie Seed
12871 380th Ave

Blue Earth, MN 56013-9608
(507) 526-3049
feder@blueearth.polaristel.net

Landscape Alternatives
1705 St Albans St
Roseville, MN 55113
(651) 488-3142

Prairie Moon Nursery
Rte 3, Box 1633
Winona, MN 55987
(507) 452-1362
pmnrsy@luminet.net
www.prairiemoonnursery.com

North American Prairies
11754 Jarvis Ave
Annandale, MN 55302
(320) 274-5316
www.northamericanprairies.com

Shooting Star Native Seed
Hwy 44 & CR 33
PO Box 648
Spring Grove, MN 55974-0648
(507) 498-3944
www.shootingstarnativeseed.com

IOWA

Ion Exchange
1878 Old Mission Rd
Harpers Ferry IA 52146
563-535-7231
hbright@means

Allendan Seed
1966 175th Lane
Winterset, IA 50273
(515) 462-1241
allendan@allendanseed.com

Cedar River Garden Center
PO Box 259
2889 Palo Marsh Rd
Palo, IA 52324
(319) 851-2161

Diversity Farms
25494 320th St
Dedham, IA 51440

(712) 683-5555
dfarms@pionet

MISSOURI

Center for Plant Conservation
Missouri Botanical Garden
4434 Shaw Blvd
PO Box 299
St Louis, MO 63166-0299
(314) 577-9400
(800) 642-8842

Missouri Native Plant Society
PO Box 20073
St Louis, MO 63144-0073

Missouri Prairie Foundation
Box 200
Columbia, MO 65205
www.moprairie.org

Shaw Nature Reserve
PO Box 38
Gray Summit, MO 63039
(636) 451-3512
www.mobot.org/shawnaturereserve

Missouri Wildflowers Nursery
9814 Pleasant Hill Rd
Jefferson City, MO 65109
(573) 496-3492
www.mowildflowers.net

EASTERN WOODLANDS FLORISTIC PROVINCE

TENNESSEE: North

Tennessee Native Plant Society
c/o Dept of Botany
U. of Tennessee
Knoxville, TN 37996-1100

KENTUCKY

Kentucky Native Plant Society
Dept of Biological Science
E. Kentucky University
Richmond, KY 40457
(859) 622-2020

Fish & Wildlife Game Farm
Nursery Greenhouse
#1 Game Farm Rd
Frankfurt, KY 40601
contact: Mary Carol Cooper
(502) 564-5280
herbs@kih.net
marycarolcooper@mail.state.ky.us

Shooting Star Nursery
444 Bates Rd
Frankfurt, KY 40601
(502) 223-1679
www.shootingstarnursery.com
shootingstarnursery@msn.com

ILLINOIS

Illinois Native Plant Society
Forest Glen Preserve
20301 E 900 North Rd
Westville, IL 61883
(217) 662-2142
ilnps@aol.com
www.inhs.uiuc.idu/inps

Wild Ones Natural Landscapers
North Park Village Nature Center
5801 N. Pulaski
Chicago, IL 60646
for local chapters info, contact:
Bob Porter
(312) 744-5472
rporter@ci.chi.org

Bluestem Prairie Nursery
13197 E. 13th Rd
Hillsboro, IL 62049
(217) 532-6344
bluestem@cillnet.com

Layfayette Home Nursery
RR 1, Box 1A
Lafayette, IL 61449
(309) 995-3311

Country Road Greenhouses
19561 E Twombly
Rochelle, IL 61068
(815) 384-3311
www.prairieplugs.com

Enders Greenhouse
104 Enders Dr
Cherry Valley, IL 61016
(815) 332-5255
endrsnatvs@aol.com

Genesis Nursery
23200 Hurd Rd
Tampico, IL 61283
(815) 438-2220

INDIANA

Indiana Native Plant and Wildflower
Society
2606 S 600 W
Morgantown, IN 46106
www.inpaws.org

Wild Ones Natural Landscapers
Gibson Woods Nature Center
6201 Parrish Ave
Hammond, IN 46323
contact Joy Bower
(219) 989-9679
jbower1126@aol.com

Hayes Regional Arboretum
801 Elks Rd
Richmond, IN 47374-2526
(765) 962-3745
www.hayesarboretum.com

Beineke's Nursery
513 Sharon Rd
West Lafayette, IN 47906
(765) 463-2994

Berg-Warner Nursery
3216 W. 850 N
Lizton, IN 46149
(317) 994-5487
bwrm@netsa1.net
www.berg-warner.com

Edge of the Prairie Wildflowers
1861 Oak Hill Rd
Crawfordsville, IN 47933
(765) 362-0915

Earthly Goods Ltd.
Ann Streckfus
PO Box 614
New Albany, IN 47150
(812) 944-2903
www.earthlygoods.com
info@earthlygoods.com

Designs on Nature
PO Box 331
Mishawaka, IN 46546
(219) 256-2242
designsonnature@hoosierlink.com

Earth Source Inc
14921 Hand Rd
Fort Wayne, IN 46818
(219) 489-8511
eric@earthsourceinc.net

MICHIGAN

Wildflower Association of Michigan
3853 Farrell Rd
Hastings, MI 49058
(616) 948 2496
wam@iserv.net
www.wildflowersmich.org

Fernwood Botanic Garden
13988 Range Line Rd
Niles, MI 49120
(616) 683-8653
www.fernwoodbotanical.org

Arrowhead Alpines
PO Box 857
Fowlerville, MI 48836
(517) 223-3581
arrowheadalpines.com
www.arrowhead-alpines.com

Hartmann's Plant Company
PO Box 100
Lacota, MI 49063-0100
(616) 253-4281
info@hartmannsplantcompany.com
www.hartmannsplantcompany.com
www.hartmannsnursery.com

WISCONSIN

The Wild Ones
Natural Landscapers, Ltd
PO Box 1274
Appleton, WI 54912-1274
For local chapters:
(877) 394-9453
www.for-wild.com

Kinnickinnic Natives
235 State Rd 65
River Falls, WI 54022
(715) 425-7605

University of Wisconsin Arboretum
1207 Seminole Hwy
Madison, WI 53711
(608) 263-7888

Schlitz Audubon Center
1111 E Brown Deer Rd
Milwaukee, WI 53217
(414) 352-2880

Wehr Nature Center
9701 W College Ave
Franklin, WI 53132
(414) 425-8550
www.countyparks.com/horticulture

Agrecol Corporation
2918 Agriculture Dr
Madison, WI 53718
(608) 825-9765
fax: (608) 825-9398

Bluestem Farm
S. 5920 Lehman Rd
Baraboo, WI 53913
(608) 356-0179
bluestem_farm@juno.com

CRM Ecosystems Inc
Prairie Ridge Nursery
9738 Overland Rd
Mt. Horeb, WI 53572
(608) 437-5245
crmeco@chorus.net

Prairie Nursery
PO Box 306
W 5875 Dyke Ave
Westfield, WI 53964
(608) 296-3679
www.prairienursery.com

OHIO

Ohio Native Plant Society
6 Louise Dr
Chagrin Falls, OH 44022

Wild Ones Native Landscaping
Inniswood Metropolitan Park
Innis House
940 S Hampstead Rd
Westerville, OH 43081
contact: Mike Hall
(614) 939-9273
mrhallblacklick@hotmail.com

Native Plant Society of Northeastern
Ohio
640 Cherry Park Oval
Aurora, OH 44202

Cherryhill Aquatics
2627 N. County Line Rd
Sunbury, OH 43074
(740) 965-2798
www.cherryhillaquatics.com
dch2627@aol.com

CONNECTICUT

Broken Arrow Nursery
13 Broken Arrow Rd
Hamden, CT 06518
(203) 288-1026
brokenarrow@snet.net
www.brokenarrownursery.com

DISTRICT OF COLUMBIA

Kenilworth Aquatic Gardens
1500 Anacostia Ave NE
Washington, DC 20020
(202) 426-6905
hps.gov/nace/keaq

Botanical Society of Washington
Department of Systematic
Biology-Botany
National Museum of Natural History
MRC 166
Smithsonian Institution
Washington, D.C. 20056
(202) 786-2995
www.si.edu

MASSACHUSETTS

New England Wild Flower Society
180 Hemenway Rd
Framingham, MA 01701-2699
(508) 877-7630
newfs@newfs.org
www.newfs.org

F.W. Schumacher Co
PO Box 1023
Sandwich, MA 02563
(508) 888-0695
www.treeshrubseed.com

Tripple Brook Farm
37 Middle Rd
Southampton, MA 10173
(413) 527-4626
info@tripplebrookfarm.com
www.tripplebrookfarm, com

NEW YORK

Wild Ones Natural Landscapers
Members Room
Brooklyn Botanic Garden
1000 Washington Ave
Brooklyn, NY 11225
(718) 768-5488
contact: Robert Saffer
(212) 314-6095
wassaffer@mindspring.com

Brooklyn Botanic Garden
1000 Washington Ave
Brooklyn, NY 11225
(718) 398-2400
lorigold@bbg.org
www.bbg.org

Cooperative Sanctuary Program
Audubon Intl
46 Rarick Rd
Selkirk, NY 12158
(518) 767-9051
www.audubonintl.org

The Fingers Lakes Native Plant
Society of Ithaca
532 Cayuga Heights Rd
Ithaca, NY 14850
(607) 257-4853

Quaker Hill Native Plant Garden
20 Dewey Lane
PO Box 667
Pawling, NY 12564
(845) 855-1531, ext 130
QHGardenoffice1@aol.com

NEW JERSEY

The Native Plant Society
of New Jersey
PO Box 231, Cook College
New Brunswick, NJ 08903-0231

Fairweather Gardens
PO Box 330
Greenwich, NJ 08323
(856) 451-6261
www.fairweathergardens.com

Toadshade Wildflower Farm
53 Everittstown Rd
Frenchtown, NJ 08825
(908) 996-7500
www.toadshade.com

PENNSYLVANIA

Pennsylvania Native Plant Society
PO Box 281
State College, PA 16804-0281
contact@pawildflower.org
www.pawildflower.org

Botanical Society of Western
Pennsylvania
5837 Nicholson St
Pittsburgh, PA 15217

Ernst Conservation Seeds
9006 Mercer Pike
Meadville, PA 16335
(814) 336-2402
(800) 336-5191
ernstseeds.co

Natural Landscapes Nursery
354 North Jennersville Rd
West Grove, PA 19390
(610) 869-3788

Noback's Farm Nursery
5943 Wool Mill Rd
Glenville, PA 17329
(717) 235-0419

Deleware Valley Fern &
Wildflower Society
263 Hillcrest Rd
Wayne, PA 19087

Appalachian Wildflower Nursery
Rte 1, Box 274A
Reedsville, PA 17084
(717) 667-6998

Bowman's Hill Wildflower Preserve
1635 River Rd
New Hope, PA 18938
(215) 862-2924
davis@bhwp.org
www.bhwp.org

Native Plant Propagation Center
580 Meetinghouse Rd
Ambler, PA 19002
(215) 283-1611

Brandywine Conservancy
Wildflower & Native Plant Gardens
PO 141, Rte 1
Chadds Ford, PA 19317
(610) 388-2700
www.brandywinemuseum.org

Shenk's Ferry Wildflower Preserve
9 New Village Rd
Holtwood, PA 17532
(717) 284-2278

Doyle Farm Nursery
158 Norris Rd
Delta, PA 17314
(717) 862-3134

Meadowbrook Farm
1633 Washington Lane
Box 3007
Meadowbrook, PA 19046
(215) 887-5900
meadow1633@aol.com
www.meadowbrook-farm.com

Sylva Native Nursery
3815 Roser Rd
Glen Rock, PA 17327
(717) 227-0486
plants@sylvanative.com
www.sylvanative.com

ONTARIO

North American Native Plant
Society
Box 84, Station D
Etobicoke, ON M9A 4X1
(416) 631-4438
nanps@nanps.org

Canadian Wildflower Society
East Toronto
43 Anaconda Ave
Scarborough, ON M1L 4M1

Canadian Wildflower Society
Dogtooth-Wellington
Botany Dept., U. of Guelph
Guelph, ON N1G 2W1

Canadian Wildflower Society
1 Windsor Cresc
London, ON N6C 1V6

Otter Valley Nursery
Gail Rhynard
Box 31, RR1
Eden, ON N0J 1H0
(519) 866-5639
otterva@kanservu.ca

Pterophylla
Mary Gartshore & Peter Carson

RR 1
Walsingham, ON N0E 1X0
(519) 586-3985
fax: (519) 586-2926
gartcar@kwic.com

Gardens North
5984 3rd Line Rd N
North Gower, ON K0A 2T0
(613) 489-0065
fax: (613) 489-1208
www.gardensnorth.com

Aimers Seeds
126 Catherine St N
Hamilton, ON L8R 1J4
(905) 529-2601
aimers.seed@sympatico.ca

Dominion Seed House
PO Box 2500
Georgetown, ON L7G 5L6
(905) 873-3037
(800) 784-3037
comment@dominion-seed-
house.com
www.dominion-seed-house.com

Humber Nurseries
RR 8
Brampton, ON L6T 3Y7
(416) 798-8733
www.humbernurseries.on.ca

William Dam Seeds
PO Box 8400
Dundas, ON L9H 6M1
(905) 628-6641
www.damseeds.com

Florabunda Seeds
PO Box 3
Indian River, ON K0L 2B0
www.florabunda.com

Grand Moraine Growers
7369 12th Line, RR 2
Alma, ON N0B 1A0
(519) 638-1101
pems@sentex.net
www.sentex.net/~pems/

Sweet Grass Gardens
RR 6
Hagersville, ON N0A 1H0
(519) 445-4828
www.sweetgrassgardens.com
info@sweetgrassgardens.com

Tallgrass Ontario
659 Exeter Rd
London, ON N6E 1L3
(519) 873-4631
www.tallgrassontario.org
info@tallgrassontario.org

Ontario Native Plant Company
Carl Hall Rd
Downsview, ON M3K 2B7
(416) 823-4627

WILD Canada
#75 - 39th St N
Wasaga Beach, ON L0L 2P0
(705) 429-4936
info@wildcanada.ca
fax: (705) 446-0822
www.wildcanada.ca

QUEBEC

Windmill Point Farms
2103 Perrot Blvd
Notredame, Ile Perrot, PQ J7V 8P4
(514) 453-9757

NOVA SCOTIA

Nova Scotia Wild Flora Society
Nova Scotia Museum
1747 Summer St
Halifax, NS B3H 3A6

PRINCE EDWARD ISLAND

McPhail Woods
RR 3
Belfast, PEI C0A 1A0
(902) 651-2575
www3.pei.simpatico.ca/
~garyschnieder
garyschnieder@pei.sympatico.ca

NEWFOUNDLAND

The Wildflower Society of
Newfoundland & Labrador
PO Box 23012
Churchill Square Post Office
St John's, NF A1B 4J9
www.ucs.mun.ca/~hclase/wf

Murray's Horticultural Services
PO Box 601
1525 Portugal Cove
Portugal Cove, NF A1M 3R6
(709) 895-2800
murraygc@nfld.com

COASTAL PLAINS FLORISTIC PROVINCE

DELAWARE

Mount Cuba Center for the Study of
Native Piedmont Flora
PO Box 3570
Greenville, DE 19807

MARYLAND

Maryland Native Plant Society
PO Box 4877
Silver Spring, MD 20914
www.mdflora.org

Fiddler's Green Nursery
3907 Old Taneytown Rd
Taneytown, MD 21787
(410) 751-0424

Kollar Environmental Service
5200 West Heaps Rd
Pylesville, MD 21132
(410) 836-0500

Lower Marlboro Nursery
PO Box 1013
Dunkirk, MD 20754
(301) 812-0808
mssds@erols.com

Wildlife Landscapes
14812 Jarretsville Pike
Monkton, MD 21111
(410) 667-9453
wildland@erols.com

VIRGINIA

Virginia Native Plant Society
Blandy Experimental Farm
Rte 2, PO Box 214
Boyce, VA 22620

Sunshine Farm & Garden
HC67 Box 539B
Renick, WV 24966
(304) 497-2208
barry@sunfarm.com
www.sunfarm.com

Enchanter's Garden
HC77 Box 108
Hinton, WV 25951
(304) 466-3134

West Virginia Native Plant Society
PO Box 75403
Charleston, WV 25375-0403

NORTH CAROLINA

North Carolina Wildflower
Preservation Society
North Carolina Botanical Garden
Totten Garden Center
3375 U. of N. Carolina
Chapel Hill, NC 27599-3375

Niche Gardens
1111 Dawson Rd
Chapel Hill, NC 27516
(919) 967-0078
fax: (919) 967-0078
www.nichegardens.com

SOUTH CAROLINA

South Carolina Native Plant Society
PO Box 759
Pickens, SC 29671
www.clemson.edu/scnativeplants

Woodlanders Inc
1128 Colleton Ave
Aiken, SC 29801
(803) 648-7522
www.woodlanders.net

S. TENNESSEE

Tennessee Native Plant Society
c/o Dept. of Botany
U. of Tennessee
Knoxville, TN 37996-1100

Sunlight Gardens
Rte 1, Box 600-A
Andersonville, TN 37705
(865) 494-8237

ARKANSAS

Arkansas Native Plant Society
PO Box 250250
Little Rock, AR 72225
(870) 460-1165 or 460-1066
sundell@uamont.edu
www.anps.org

Arkansas Arboretum
Pinnacle Mountain State Park
11901 Pinnacle Valley Rd
Roland, AR 72135
(501) 868-5806

Pine Ridge Gardens
Mary Ann King
PO Box 200
London, AR 72847
(501) 293-4359

E. TEXAS

Native Plant Society of Texas
PO Box 891
Georgetown, TX 78627-0891
www.npsot.org

Mercer Arboretum & Botanic
Garden
22306 Aldine-Westfield Rd
Humble, TX 77338
(713) 443-8731

Lynn's Landscaping, Inc
2060 Pecan Orchard Rd
League City, TX 77573
(281) 332-4651
tony@houston.rr.com
www.lynnslandscaping.com

Lilyponds Water Gardens
839 FM 1489
Brookshire, TX 77423
(713) 934-8525

Ecovirons
10290 Hummingbird Pl
Conroe, TX 77385
(281) 362-1107
cyrilla@flex.netwww.ecovirons.com

The Lowrey Nursery
2323 Sleepy Hollow Rd
Conroe, TX 77385
(936) 449-4040

LOUISIANA

Louisiana Native Plant Society
216 Caroline Dormon Rd
Saline, LA 71070

Lafayette Natural History Museum
637 Girard Park Dr
Lafayette, LA 70504
(337) 291-5544

Gulf Coast Plantsmen
15680 Perkins Rd
Baton Rouge, LA 70810
(225) 751-0395

Louisiana Nursery
RTE 7, Box 43
Opelousas, LA 70570
(337) 948-3696

MISSISSIPPI

The Mississippi Native Plant Society
Mississippi Museum of Natural
Science
111 North Jefferson St
Jackson, MS 39201
(601) 354-7303

The Crosby Arboretum
3702 Hardy St
Hattiesburg, MS 39402
(601) 799-2311

ALABAMA

Auburn University Arboretum
Garden Street
Auburn, AL 36830
(334) 844-5770

Birmingham Botanical Garden
2612 Lane Park Rd
Birmingham, AL 35223
(205) 414-3900

GEORGIA

Georgia Native Plant Society
PO Box 422085
Atlanta, GA 30342-2085
(770) 343-6000
www.gnps.org
gnps@mindspring.com

Georgia Southern University
Botanical Garden
1211 Fair Rd
Statesboro, GA 30458
(912) 871-1114

Goodness Grows
332 Elberton Rd
Lexington, GA 30648
(706) 743-5055

Atlanta Botanical Garden
1345 Piedmont Ave NE
Atlanta, GA 30309
(404) 876-5859
www.atlantabotanicalgarden.org

Transplant Nursery Inc
1586 Parkertown Rd
Lavonia, GA 30553
(706) 356-8947

FLORIDA

Florida Native Plant Society
PO Box 690278
Vero Beach, FL 32969-0278
fax: (561) 562-1598
www.fnps.org

That Native Plant Place
1112 Sanctuary Rd
Naples, FL 34120
(941) 348-1093
tech@thatnativeplantplace.com
www.thatnativeplantplace.com

Florida Native Plants Inc
730 Myakka Rd
Sarasota, FL 34240
(941) 322-1915
www.floridanativeplants.com

Green Images / Native Landscape
Plants
1333 Taylor Creek Rd
Christmas, FL 32709
(407) 568-1333
greenimage@aol.com

Indian Trails Native Nursery
6315 Park Lane Rd W
Lakeworth, FL 33467-6606
(561) 641-9488
IndianTrails@afnn.org
www.afnn.org/indiantrails.htm

The Natives Inc
2929 JB Carter Rd
Davenport, FL 33837
(863) 422-6664
natives@gate.net

All Native Garden Center
300 Center Rd
Ft. Meyers, FL 33907-1513
(941) 939-9663
no-lanw@iline.com

Native Nurseries
1661 Centerville Rd
Tallahassee, FL 32308
(850) 386-8882

TRUE NORTH

ALASKA

Alaska Native Plant Society
PO Box 141613
Anchorage, AK 99514-1613
(907) 333-8212
akkrafts@alaskakrafts.com

Georgeson Botanical Garden
U. of Alaska at Fairbanks
West Tanana Dr
PO Box 757200
Fairbanks, AK 99775-7200
(907) 474-5651

YUKON TERRITORIES

Arctic Alpine Seed
105 Granite Rd
Whitehorse, YK Y1A 2V8
(867) 667-2756

Further Reading

GENERAL

Druse, Ken. *The Natural Garden.* New York: Clarkson Potter, 1989.

Hightshoe, Gary. *Native Trees, Shrubs, and Vines for Urban and Rural America.* New York: John Wiley, 1988.

Holmes, Roger, ed. *Taylor's Guide to Natural Gardening.* Boston: Houghton Mifflin, 1993.

Johnson, Lorraine. *100 Easy to Grow Native Plants for Canadian Gardens.* Toronto: Random House, 1999.

Johnson, Lorraine. *Grow Wild! Native-Plant Gardening in Canada and Northern United States.* Toronto: Random House, 1998.

Knopf, Jim, Sally Wasowski, John K. Boring, Glenn Keator, Jane Scott, and Erica Glasener. *Natural Gardening, A Nature Company Guide.* New York: Time-Life Books, 1995.

Niering, William, and Nancy Olmstead. *The Audubon Society Field Guide to North American Wildflowers, Eastern Region.* New York: Alfred A. Knopf, 1990.

Spellenberg, Richard. *The Audubon Society Field Guide to North American Wildflowers, Western Region.* New York: Alfred A. Knopf, 1990.

Stein, Sara. *Noah's Garden: Restoring the Ecology of Our Own Back Yards.* Boston: Houghton Mifflin, 1993.

Stein, Sara. *Planting Noah's garden: Further Adventures in Backyard Ecology.* Boston: Houghton Mifflin, 1997.

Wasowski, Sally. *Requiem for a Lawn Mower (and Other Essays on Easy Gardening with Native Plants).* Dallas: Taylor Publishing Company, 1992.

GARDENING FOR WILDLIFE

Degraaf, Richard, and Gretchen M. Witman. *Trees, Shrubs and Vines for Attracting Birds: A Manual for the Northeast.* Amherst: University of Massachusetts Press, 1979.

Dennis, John V. *The Wildlife Gardener.* New York: Knopf, 1985.

Gunnarson, L., and F. Haselsteiner, eds., The Xerxes Society/Smithsonian Institution. *Butterfly Gardening: Creating Summer Magic in Your Garden.* San Francisco: Sierra Club Books and National Wildlife Federation Books, 1990.

Tekulsky, Mathew. *The Hummingbird Garden.* New York: Crown, 1990.
Tufts, Craig. *The Backyard Naturalist.* Washington: National Wildlife Federation, 1988.

CALIFORNIA FLORISTIC PROVINCE

Connelly, Kevin. *Gardener's Guide to California Wildflowers.* Sun Valley: Theodore Payne Foundation, 1991.
Keator, Glenn. *Complete Garden Guide to the Native Perennials of California.* San Francisco: Chronicle Books, 1990.
Keator, Glenn. *Complete Guide to Native Shrubs of California.* San Francisco: Chronicle Books, 1994.
Schmidt, Marjorie. *Growing California Native Plants.* Berkeley: University of California Press, 1980.

THE PACIFIC NORTHWEST

Grant, John A., and Carol L. Grant. *Trees and Shrubs for Pacific Northwest Gardens* Portland, Oregon: Timber Press, 1990.
Hitchcock, C. Leo, and Arthur Cronquist. *Flora of the Pacific Northwest: An Illustrated Manual.* Seattle: University of Washington Press, 1973.
Kruckeberg, Arthur R. *Gardening with Native Plants of the Pacific Northwest: An Illustrated Guide.* Vancouver/Toronto Douglas & McIntyre, 1982.
Perry, Robert C. *Landscape Plants for Western Regions.* Claremont: Land Design Publishing, 1992.
Pettinger, April. *Native Plants in the Coastal Garden: A Guide for Gardeners in British Columbia and the Pacific Northwest.* Vancouver: Whitecap, 1998.
Spellenberg, Richard. *The Audubon Society Field Guide to North American Wild Flowers.* New York: Chanticleer Press, 1979.

THE WESTERN MOUNTAINS AND BASINS

Kershaw, Linda J., Jim Pojar, and Paul Alaback. *Plants of the Rocky Mountains.* Edmonton: Lone Pine Publishing, 1998.
Knopf, Jim. *The Xeriscape Flower Gardener: A Waterwise Guide for the Rocky Mountain Region.* Boulder: Johnson Books, 1991.
Moore, Michael. *Medicinal Plants of the Mountain West.* Albuquerque: Museum of New Mexico Press, 1989.
Porsild, A.E. *Rocky Mountain Wild Flowers.* Ottawa: National Museums of Canada, 1979.
Van Bruggen, Theodore. *Wildflowers, Grasses, and Other Plants of the Northern Great Plains.* Interior: Badlands Natural History Association, 1983.

THE SOUTHWESTERN DESERTS

Benson, Lyman, and Robert A. Darrow. *Trees and Shrubs of the Southwestern Deserts*. Tuscon: University of Arizona Press, 1981.

Buchanan, Rita, and Roger Holmes, eds. *Taylor's Guide to Gardening in the Southwest*. Boston: Houghton Mifflin, 1992.

Kearney, Thomas, and Robert Peebles. *Arizona Flora*. Berkeley: University of California Press, 1960.

Phillips, Judith. *Southwestern Landscaping with Native Plants*. Santa Fe: Museum of New Mexico Press, 1987.

Sunset Western Garden Book. Menlo Park: California Lane Publishing Company, 1979.

Wasowski, Sally, and Andy Wasowski. *Native Gardens for Dry Climates*. New York: Clarkson N. Potter, 1995.

THE GREAT PLAINS

Barr, Claude A. *Jewels of the Plains: Wildflowers of the Great Plains Grasslands and Hills*. Minneapolis: University of Minnesota Press, 1983.

Curragh, R., A. Smreciu, and M. Van Dyk. *Prairie Wildflowers*. Edmonton: University of Alberta, 1983.

Morgan, John, Doug R. Collicutt, and Jacqueline J. Tompson. *Restoring Canada's Native Prairies, A Practical Manual*. Argyle: Prairie Habitats, 1995.

Packard, Stephen, and Cornelia F. Matel, eds. *The Tallgrass Restoration Handbook: For Prairies, Savannas and Woodlands*. Washington: Island Press, 1996.

Smith, J. Robert, and Beatrice S. Smith. *The Prairie Garden: 70 Native Plants You Can Grow in Town or Country*. Madison: University of Wisconsin Press, 1980.

The Wild Ones Natural Landscapers Handbook. www: The Wild Ones Natural Landscapers, Inc., 1998-2001.

Wasowski, Sally, and Andy Wasowski. *Native Texas Plants: Landscaping Region by Region*. Austin: Texas Monthly Press, 1988.

Wasowski, Sally, and Julie Ryan. *Landscaping with Native Texas Plants*. Austin: Texas Monthly Press, 1984.

THE EASTERN WOODLANDS

Art, Henry W. *The Wildflower Gardener's Guide: Northeast, Mid-Atlantic, Great Lakes, and Eastern Canada Edition*. Pownal: Storey, 1987.

Birdseye, Clarence, and Eleanor Birdseye. *Growing Woodland Plants*. New York: Dover, 1972.

Brumbrack, William E., and David Longland. *Garden In The Woods Cultivation Guide*. Framingham: New England Wildflower Society, 1986.

Burrell, C. Colston. *Ferns: Wild Things Make a Comeback in the Garden*. Brooklyn: Brooklyn Botanic Garden, 1994.

Flint, H.L. *Landscape Plants for Eastern North America.* New York: John Wiley, 1983.

Meadows and Meadow Gardening. Framingham: New England Wildflower Society, 1990.

Native Plants for Woodland Gardens: Selection, Design and Culture. Framingham: New England Wildflower Society, 1987.

THE COASTAL PLAINS

Brown, C.L., and L.K. Kirkman. *Trees of Georgia and Adjacent States.* Portland: Timber Press, 1989.

Buchanan, Rita, and Roger Holmes, eds. *Taylor's Guide to Gardening in the South.* Boston: Houghton Mifflin, 1992.

Duncan, Wilbur H., and Leonard Foote. *Wildflowers of the Southeastern United States.* Athens: University of Georgia Press, 1975.

Foote, Leonard, and Samuel B. Jones, Jr. *Native Shrubs and Woody Vines of the Southeast: Landscaping Uses and Identification.* Portland: Timber Press, 1989.

Halfacre, R.G., and A.R. Showcroft. *Landscape Plants of the Southeast.* Raleigh: Sparks Press, 1989.

Wigginton, B.E. *Trees and Shrubs of the Southeast.* Athens: University of Georgia Press, 1963.

Index

thistle sage (*Salvia carduacea*), 80
Thuidium delicatulum (fern moss),
129
Thuja plicata (western red cedar), 14
Tiarella cordifolia var. *collina*
(foamflower), 129
tiger lily, 83
torry mesquite, 101
toyon (*Heteromeles arbutifolia*), 61,
63, 81
Tradescantia ohiensis (Ohio spiderwort), 71
trumpet creeper (*Campsis radicans*), 65, 118
trumpet vine (*Bignonia capreolata*),
62
Tsuga canadensis (hemlock), 62
Turk's cap (*Malvaviscus drummondii*), 18
Turk's-cap lily (*Lilium superbum*),
120
turkey foot (big bluestem
Andropogon gerardii), 52, 60,
110, 111, 115, 130

Vaccinium ovatum (evergreen
huckleberry), 88
VanDeKerckhove garden, 119
van Veenendaal garden, 35, 83
Verbena bonariensis (verbena), 60
Verbena canadensis (rose verbena),
61, 114, 132
Viguiera multiflora (showy golden-
eye), 94
Viola glabella (stream-side violet),
29
Viola palustra (marsh violet), 84
violet (*Viola* spp.) , 29, 61, 84, 123
Vitis riparia (riverbank grape), 98
Virginia bluebell (*Mertensia virgini-
ca*), 62, 65, 119, 123
Virginia creeper (*Parthenocissus
quinquefolia*), 62

water consumption, 11–13
watering plants, 17, 27, 49, 77–78,
103, 112

water lily, white-flowered, 130
water pollution, 14–15
water tupelo, 130
wax myrtle (*Myrica cerifera*), 130,
135
weeds, 21, 27
western azalea, 83
western bleeding heart (*Dicentra
formosa*), 86
western blue flag (*Iris
missouriensis*), 42, 63, 93
western flowering dogwood (Pacific
flowering dogwood *Cornus nuttallii*), 89
western hemlock, 83
Western Mountains and Basins
Floristic Province, 90–98; native
plants, 42, 63–64, 91, 92; plant
resources, 142–46
western red cedar (*Thuja plicata*),
14
western yarrow (*Achillea millefolium*), 109
white-flowered water lily, 130
wild bergamot (*Monarda fistulosa*),
44–45, 52, 53, 71, 73, 116
wild blue indigo (*Baptisia australis*
var. *australis*), 125
wild buckwheat (*Eriogonum* spp.),
80
wild columbine (*Aquilegia
canadensis*), 62, 65, 122
wildflower gardens, 69–71
wild four o'clock (*Mirabilis multiflora*), 93
wild ginger (*Asarum canadense*),
133
wildlife, garden, 28, 59
wild lilac (*Ceanothus* spp.), 81
wild monardo (wild bergamot
Monarda fistulosa), 116
*Wild Ones Natural Landscapers'
Handbook, The*, 70–71
wild onion, 61
wild red mallow, 130
wild rye, Canada (*Elymus canadensis*), 52

Photo: Chris Staples

Carole Rubin is the best-selling author of *How to Get Your Lawn & Garden Off Drugs: Pesticide-free Gardening for a Healthier Environment.* Rubin is a past director of the West Coast Environmental Law Association, past chairperson and co-ordinator of the BC Coalition for Alternatives to Pesticides, and the Canadian Environmental Network's Alternatives to Pesticides Caucus. The alarming waste of drinking water on North American lawns prompted her to come out of 'retirement' to write this book. She lives on the Sunshine Coast of British Columbia, where she grows organic herbs and vegetables and tends to the native plants in her yard, which she never, ever waters.